Holy Things
for Youth Ministry

Holy Things
for Youth Ministry

13 Practical Lessons

BRIAN HARDESTY-CROUCH

THE
PILGRIM
PRESS
Cleveland

The Pilgrim Press
700 Prospect Avenue
Cleveland, Ohio 44115-1100
thepilgrimpress.com

ISBN-13: 978-0-8298-1853-6

14 13 12 11 10   5 4 3 2 1

Contents

Part Three
TABLE

Part Four
TIME

Appendix
SUPPLEMENTAL
MATERIALS

Preface

We believe in you! And we believe you have a youth ministry that matters! Beneath these acclamations are these foundational beliefs:

- We believe in God, revealed in Jesus Christ, by the power of the Holy Spirit.
- We believe that worship is a central practice of the Christian life.
- We believe Christian worship is a source and resource for how we live and how we are in ministry.
- We believe youth ministry matters!

Every session in this book is written by someone who has given a part of themselves in ministry with teenagers. Each contributor holds that special combination: a deep faith that is lived out in real-life ministry. They are youth workers, schoolteachers, writers, speakers, professors, clergy, social workers, and pastors.

Each contributor has degrees, credentials, and initials; but that's probably not why you're buying this book. What's more significant is that each writer has been a part of an amazing ministry that offers deeper roots to youth ministry (on the Duke Youth Academy see page 241 below). If you believe God wants to strengthen or grow your youth ministry, it's got to have good, strong roots. As contributors we've all been challenged, changed, and strengthened in ministry through the approaches offered in this resource. We believe you and the youth with whom you minister will be transformed as well, because it is God who gives the growth (1 Corinthians 3:5–9). Many, many thanks for your effort and this invitation to share in ministry. I believe many will be blessed!

Christianity has tools to till the soil where faith in Christ grows. We have windows and doorways into the mystery of God's love in Jesus Christ. Led by Dr. Fred Edie, we call these book, bath, table, and time.

That's Scripture, baptism, Eucharist/Holy Communion, and God's time reflected in practices like Sabbath-keeping and the Christian calendar. Yet often, especially in congregational youth ministry, we have skipped over exploring these foundational mysteries in pursuit of today's "hot topic." Amazingly, right out of these key components of worship come direction for and insight into how to live as a follower of Jesus Christ for a myriad of life's "hot topics!"

Through this resource you can lead the youth of your community to deeper faith and more joyful living as they discover who they are, whose they are, and what God calls them to do. There are several ways that this resource can be used:

+ Weekly for a quarter of the year

+ Once a month

+ On retreat or a series of retreats

+ When God nudges you

+ Whenever you want an interesting faith experience for the youth you serve

This work, like yours, is offered for the glory of God. With gratitude, I'd like to also offer these words of appreciation:

Thank you to the community of the Duke Youth Academy for Christian Formation: participants, fellows, staff, and faculty, as well as our service and hospitality partners in congregations and communities. Thank you to all those parents, families, pastors, youth, and youth workers who trusted and helped us while an idea became an experience over this first decade.

None of this project would have happened this way without generous support from Lilly Endowment, Inc., and Duke Endowment. Thank you! Thanks also to the people of The Pilgrim Press.

I'd like to thank Janice Virtue and the dream team who helped to begin this journey, as well as the supportive leadership, faculty and staff of Duke Divinity School at Duke University, including Richard Hays, L. Gregory Jones, Dave Odom, Cindy Monteith, Brian Jones, Elizabeth Ingram Schindler, Fred Edie, and Katherine Smith. Fred's and Katherine's gifts for ministry and leadership give shape to the current life of the Duke Youth Academy. My life and ministry is but one of many shaped by their leadership.

I thank God for the Holy Moments Board, HeartPaths Spirituality Centre, and the Sabbath Group where life and ministry are shared. I appreciate the North Texas Conference of the United Methodist Church and its colleagues and structures that support creative ministries.

A big thank you to my family (especially MB), friends, and colleagues who are encouraging and supportive for time spent with DYA and related projects. You are a blessing.

—BHC

Note: In the Leaders Preparation section for each session, we have included horizontal lines for writing short responses to the questions listed. These lines are to invite and encourage you to actually pause to prepare spiritually by writing down your prayers, thoughts, and insights. The questions are not meant to be just rhetorical nor are they designed to "breeze by."

The handouts in the appendix are meant to be photocopied and distributed. The line on these handouts are for the participants.

Part One

BOOK

Session 1

Reading the Bible
as God's "Story of Salvation"
Fred P. Edie

LEADER PREPARATION

Prepare Your Soul

Devotion

A mom once reported to me this fascinating interchange with her college student daughter. While daughter sat at the kitchen table late one Saturday afternoon preparing a Bible study for the next morning, Mom nagged her, saying: "We need to pick up that bride's maid dress at the mall before it closes. When else will we find time to do it?" After two or three more such invocations the daughter rolled her eyes at her mother and responded, "Mother, can't you see that I am listening to the Lord's words?" The mom recognized immediately how cleverly her daughter had located them both within a biblical story, the daughter playing Mary to her own chastened Martha.

Read the story of Mary and Martha in Luke 10:38 – 42.

What grabs you in this story?

_____

_____

What stories enliven you, chasten you, fill you with hope, or help you make sense of your life?

_____

_____

_____

How do these stories shape your imagination and the ways you interpret the world?

_____

_____

_____

Consciously or not, stories *do* animate our imaginations and our very lives. Not only do stories shape us, however; we ourselves are storied beings. If an interviewer were to ask you to describe yourself, anything more than the briefest of answers would involve telling a story that has become the story of who you are.

When you meet someone or make a new friend, what stories do you tell to communicate who you are?

_____

_____

_____

How do you feel about your part in God's Story of Salvation?

_____

_____

_____

What stories do you tell to convey how Jesus Christ matters to you?

_____

_____

_____

Prepare Your Mind

Until recently, sophisticated moderns have believed stories to be merely child's play. The church, for example, while delighting in teaching its stories to children, sometimes shifts to an emphasis upon "universal meanings" behind stories when teaching youth and adults. The story of Jesus' passion, for example, becomes important not for its narrative details but for its ability to capture "the existential fear of death." Several unfortunate consequences for faith formation follow from this reductionism.

First, giving up on biblical stories after childhood has meant that young Christians remain mostly illiterate when it comes to the basic narrative arc of the Christian faith. For stories to resound within us they must be so frequently repeated that we know them (and they know us) by heart. Lacking storied literacy the young unsurprisingly lack storied Christian identity as well.

> **We seek not just to "apply" the Bible to our lives, but to be swept up into the ultimate story of Jesus Christ!**

Second, our failure to cultivate storied literacy in young people has also reduced their capacities for awe, wonder, and imagination. Instead, the emphasis is placed on how the Bible may be "applied" to my life in utilitarian fashion rather than inviting young minds to the far more radical step of imagining how I may be taken up into the story of Jesus Christ.

For these reasons this session seeks to (re-)introduce students to the Bible (and themselves) as storied. It encourages them to look for a discernible plot amid all the twists and turns of seemingly random biblical episodes occurring and recorded over millennia. As a reminder, here are the basic moves:

- God creates the cosmos in love;

- God seeks redemption for fallen creation (particularly the human members of that creation) through covenants with Israel and ultimately through the life, death, and resurrection of Jesus Christ;

- God sends the Holy Spirit to animate the church as Christ's body in the world and as the principal means toward the fulfillment of God's promised Reign.

Such a plot holds implications for participants' own evolving stories:

- I am a beloved creature; I am in rebellion from God to the extent that I am in denial of either my creatureliness or my belovedness;

- I am joined to God through my baptism into the life, death, and resurrection of Jesus Christ;
- And I am privileged and called to get involved with the creation of God's Reign on Earth.

Not only is recognizing the biblical content as storied important to its proper understanding, so is its storied genre critical to recognizing the Bible's place and role in worship. When communities gather to worship they read the Bible publicly and they tell these stories of God repeatedly in order to lay claim to a clearer sense of their own identity and calling.

Story is a critical theme not only to this session but to this entire curriculum. Not only does the Bible contain the Story of God's Salvation, our practices around the bath, the table, and the patterning of time enact that Story as well. Even avowedly anti-liturgical congregations tell the story of a baby born in a manger at Christmas and the resurrection of the crucified one at Easter. The church does this to remind itself of its origins, and, more important, to animate its present and future life consistent with the Spirit's leading. Story telling, story rehearsing, story enacting — all are key to worship. Thus, this orienting session seeks to ground students in the power of Story, as a means to deepen their participation in Christian worship and to recall the contents of their own Christian Story.

Prepare Your Heart

Young people sometimes feel compelled to renounce their childhoods instead of incorporating those aspects of their being into the persons they are becoming. Thus they may resist (initially) seemingly childish exercises in exploring the Bible as Story and recalling biblical stories. But the intent of this session, in part, is to demonstrate how human beings never outgrow the power of narrative to shape imagination and form identity. Your own heartfelt openness to this possibility in your life will enable students to suspend whatever disbelief they might bring with them into the session.

Theological ethicist Stanley Hauerwas says that story and church go together. In fact, to paraphrase his central claim, the principal task of the church is to learn to live faithful to the story of Jesus

Christ. What might it mean for you and your group to imagine the Christian life as storied? And especially to the point of this session, what might it mean for you and your group to re-imagine the Bible as the unfolding Story of God's Salvation of the World?

We hope you will prepare your heart to welcome some "real characters" in God's story, your very own participants and young friends.

Prepare Your Space

For "Create a Biblical Storyline" (see page 12) you will need either to designate a blank wall where descriptions and illustrations of central biblical events may be posted in sequence or hang string or wire across the room that will be used for the same purpose. In either case you also will need something to attach the illustrations to the wall or line.

Prepare Your Supplies

- If you plan to do "Consider the Truthfulness of Stories" (page 9) secure ahead of time a copy of *The Velveteen Rabbit*.

- Bibles, drawing supplies (crayons or markers), paper, tape or other fastener.

- String or wire to span classroom from one wall to another.

Prepare Your Plan

If you use the activity "Consider the Truthfulness of Stories," practice reading *The Velveteen Rabbit* aloud before the session.

"Create a Biblical Storyline" could become an extended project of building a permanent group resource. For example, instead of a line strung across the classroom or a designated wall, participants could design a web resource to be linked to the church's website. A cover page would list the individual stories of the Story in chronological order with each story being a clickable link to in-depth student-researched explanatory content on the text and related artwork.

Prepare Your Publicity

Get the word out about this upcoming session in multiple ways. Use print, verbal, artistic, and electronic means to invite participants. You could use phrases such as "What's your story?" and "God's got a story" and "You're a character — in the story of God!"

Prepare in Prayer

Pray the Lord's Prayer (see Matthew 6:9–13) or prayerfully say the Nicene Creed or Apostles' Creed. Be mindful of the narrative shape of these Christian texts. Reflect upon how they point in condensed fashion to the broader Story of Salvation.

Prepare Further

Want to know more? *Why Narrative? Readings in Narrative Theology* (Eerdmans, 1989), edited by Duke faculty members Stanley Hauerwas and Greg Jones, is a collection of challenging essays seeking to highlight the importance of story for considerations of knowledge, human identity, and Christian theology.

The God-Hungry Imagination: The Art of Storytelling for Post-modern Youth Ministry (Upper Room, 2007), by former Duke Youth Academy artist-in-residence and contributor to this volume Sarah Arthur, imaginatively explores the value of stories and storytelling as central features in ministry with the young.

TEMPLATE FOR SESSION ONE
Reading the Bible as God's "Story of Salvation"

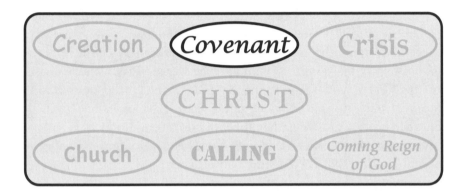

Key Scripture: Psalm 136:26

O give thanks to the God of heaven, for his steadfast love endures forever.

Objectives

- To consider the Bible as "Story" and become (re-)acquainted with essential pieces of its storyline.
- To read the Scriptures in "stories" using storied practices and then reflect upon how these practices shape interpretations of Scripture.
- To be invited to reflect on the connections between God's unfolding Story of Salvation and the participants' own emerging life stories.

Appetizer A:
Consider the Truthfulness of Stories (20–30 minutes)

Invite your participants to join you in prayer:

Leader: The Lord be with you.

Group: And also with you.

Leader: Let us pray. Storied God, you seek to make us characters in your unfolding drama of salvation. Teach us your own Story and write upon our lives stories that aspire to your truth, your justice, and your beauty. We pray through Jesus Christ and in the power of the Holy Spirit. Amen.

Say: "Today we begin [or resume] our study of Christian life through the lens of worship. Through this study I hope you will find the means to worship God more faithfully, understand worship with more mature insight, and discover how worship seeks to form us as Christ's body for service to God and the world. This session focuses on the Bible in worship, in particular on how the Bible contains God's Story of Salvation, a story we tell at least part of in one form or another every time we gather for worship. In addition, this session invites you to consider your own life as an unfolding and not yet complete story that is somehow tied up with God's Story.

> Tip: Because the preceding paragraph states some goals of this session, write some key words for all to see, such as "Bible in worship," "God's Story of Salvation," and "Our story tied up with God's Story."

"For the next few moments I will read you a story called *The Velveteen Rabbit.* I know listening to a story read aloud is a practice you may not have indulged in for quite some time. Your job is to relax quietly and listen imaginatively. When I'm finished I'll invite your reflections on the *content* of the story and also upon the *practice* of storytelling."

Read the Story

Ask questions like these:

* Is this a story you know from childhood? If so, what is it like to hear it again years later? How has your perspective changed?

* Is this story true? In what ways?

(Responses may point to the truth that "real" life may mean becoming acquainted with suffering borne of love.)

* Now a question about the practice of storytelling: How is sharing the story of *The Velveteen Rabbit* somehow more compelling and maybe even more true than my simply telling you that "real life and real love may involve suffering"?

(This question is intended to prompt participants to consider the evocative and formative power of narrative. Responses may include how stories appeal to the heart and the imagination, that they make no pretense to authority because they do not demand assent; that there is pleasure in participating in storytelling; that we are disarmed of our defenses by being invited to identify with the characters in a story in light of our own stories.)

* What might it mean for us to approach the Bible as Story or storied?

For a shorter session, choose either Appetizer A or Appetizer B.

Appetizer B:
Share a Family Story (8–12 minutes)

Invite participants to pair up. Allow each person a minute to tell a story about immediate or extended family to the other. This story should have some bearing on family identity. You may wish to begin the conversation with a story from your own family. (For example, my father, who grew up during the Depression, regularly told stories about neighbors and others coming to live with his family after they lost jobs or homes. Then when I was a child, the house of family friends burned down. Having heard all his stories I wasn't surprised when my dad invited them to stay with us until it was repaired.)

Reflection Questions

- What family stories seem to have shaped who you are as a family or who you are as a member of that family?
- Who are the storytellers in your extended family? Where and when do they engage in their art?
- How does the story you told about your family affect you?
- How does it shape the way you understand yourself?
- Some of you may have struggled to recall family stories. Recognizing that no one is to be blamed for this, what might be the effect of not telling, having, or knowing any family stories?

First Course:
Create a Biblical Storyline

Say: "Because the Bible contains so much material, it can be challenging to understand how it all hangs together. This exercise frames the Bible as many episodes in God's single unfolding Story of Salvation. God's Covenant Love is the theme that weaves all these stories together into one unified Story. As you may know, a covenant is a legal agreement that binds two parties together in mutual interest. Because God loves God's own creation, the Bible repeatedly witnesses to God's covenant-making, first with the people of Israel and second with the church through Jesus Christ. Though in conventional covenants both parties agree to uphold their own parts of the agreement, in the unfolding Story of Salvation, God increasingly assumes responsibility for not only God's side of the covenant but for the human side as well. Such a God is either crazy or crazy in love with creation."

Step One (10–20 minutes)

Say: "Let's look at biblical texts that contain stories of God's covenants with God's people. Be prepared to briefly summarize the covenant story you are assigned and to answer the following questions." After giving the instructions and letting participants begin, post the questions for all to see.

- How does this story express or imply covenant? What is expected of God? Of human beings?

- Is your story primarily about covenant blessing or covenant brokenness?
- What does God do in this story? What do people do?
- What if any signs or symbols of covenant are present in this story? How do these signs function?

Assign texts based on group size. In a group with many participants, form small groups to work on a single text. With fewer participants assign individual (or multiple) texts to individual students. Note that this latter method will likely require more time.

> Desired result: To encounter covenant stories in the Bible. If you have a small group or less time, assign only one story for each character.

Covenant Stories

Genesis: Creation	Genesis 2:4–24
Noah: Flood	Genesis 6:9–22
Noah: Rainbow	Genesis 9:1–17
Abraham's "Smoking Pot"	Genesis 15:7–21
Abraham: Promise and Circumcision	Genesis 17:1–27
Moses: Covenant Memory	Exodus 6:2–8
Moses: Escape from Egypt	Exodus 14:21–15:21
Moses: Wilderness Wandering	Exodus 16
Moses: Ten Commandments	Exodus 34:28; Deut. 5:1–21
Joshua: People Prepare for Promised Land	Joshua 1:1–11
Joshua: Ark of Covenant Crosses Jordan River	Joshua 3:11–17
Amos: Warnings against Covenant Unfaithfulness	Amos 5
Jeremiah: Promise of a New Covenant	Jeremiah 31:27–34; 32:40
Ezekiel: Promise of a New Covenant	Ezekiel 36:25–28
Jesus: New Covenant	Luke 22:19–21
Acts: Birth of Church	Acts 2:1–21
Revelation: Promised Reign	Revelation 21:1–7

Share findings as you have time.

Step Two (6–12 minutes)

Provide drawing materials and paper. Have students depict their story visually and label it. Then have them either tape it in proper sequence to the timeline on the wall or hang it from the line strung across the room.

> "I come from a fairly low church tradition, but DYA always shows me that liturgy, written prayers, the lectionary, etc., are both meaningful and useful in my own practice of my faith."
> — From Duke Youth Academy for Christian Formation participant (2009)

Looking at the plotline the group has created, say something like this: "Note how we have gathered in one place many of the most important stories of the Bible. Note also how the individual stories are unified into one Story by the theme of covenant: God chooses to be bound to creation in love from the very beginning to the very end. This story opens with the drama of creation, depicts God's calling of a people through Noah and Abraham, delivers this people from slavery in Egypt to the Promised Land, and then chronicles with great sadness Israel's exile in Babylon as a result of their failure to live as God's People. God promises a new beginning, however, and the story reaches a fever pitch amid the accounts of the life, death, and resurrection of Jesus Christ. Once Jesus has risen the Spirit falls upon the church to transform it into Christ's body on earth. This Spirit-empowered church is presently on a journey to the fullness of God's Reign wherein we all live 'happily ever after.' "

To reiterate say:

• This is the basic storyline of the Bible. It is essential to know this storyline because the stories tend to build upon one another. Notice, for example, how God gradually takes more and more responsibility for keeping *us* faithful to covenants to the point of taking responsibility when *we* disobey. And notice how New

Testament references to Jesus as the "New Adam" or the "New Moses" or as "paschal lamb" make sense only to the extent you know the earlier stories of Adam, of Moses, or of the Passover lambs sacrificed in order to preserve and deliver Israel (Exodus 12:21–28.)

- This story becomes our story at baptism. (See Session 6 for further details.)

- Even the parts of the Bible that are not "storied" (the laws in Leviticus, the moral sayings in Proverbs, the letters in the New Testament) are nonetheless devoted to reflecting upon what it means to live into the biblical Story or instructing us on how to so live.

- The Story is not finished yet. We are way past "once upon a time" but have not arrived at "and they all lived happily ever after." Like members of an improv troupe, you are invited to enter into the story of what God is doing in the world and help bring it to its intended end. The better you know the story to this point, the easier for you to "get into character" for the role you are to play. (Sorry, it's still a small role; God is the main character! And isn't Jesus a "star"? Revelation 22:16).

Second Course:
Practice Reading the Bible as Story (12–20 minutes)

Read 1 Samuel 16:1–13 as "Readers' Theater." Let participants who enjoy reading publicly volunteer to take the roles of Narrator, God, Samuel, and Jesse. The rest of the group can stand in for the Elders of Bethlehem. *Note:* You can help the volunteer Narrator be prepared to pronounce names such as Jesse, Eliab, Abinadab, Shammah, and David. If you like, utilize a Bible dictionary. Invite readers to stand at the front of the room facing the group. Read the text in this way:

Narrator:　　The Lord said to Samuel,

God:　　How long will you grieve over Saul...

Narrator:　　And Samuel said,

Samuel:　　How can I go? ...

If the group is large, form discussion groups of four to six. You may designate a participant as the convenor of each group.

When readers have finished, ask questions like these:

- How does engaging the Bible this way compare or contrast with reading it silently to yourself?

- What are the narrative features of this passage, e.g., plot, characters, building tension, repetition, climactic resolution?

- Of what other biblical stories does this story remind you?

- How does this story fit into the wider biblical Story of God's Salvation? What persons or events have come before it? What will follow it?

- How does this story evoke something of your own experience? How does it feel to be chosen/not chosen? (note the potential intersection of Biblical Story and personal stories)

- How is God's choosing similar to or different from your experiences of choosing? What kinds of people does God call in the Old Testament?

- How might God be calling you to serve God? (invitation to respond to a story with a story)

Dessert: Worship (3–10 minutes)

Read Psalm 136 responsively.

Desired result: To celebrate God's Story in worship.

Set a worshipful tone by moving to a worship space, dimming the lights, lighting a candle, or singing.

Select one student to read aloud the first half of each verse in this Psalm. All will respond: "for God's steadfast love endures forever." After the reading, pray:

O God, we give thanks for this Story of your steadfast love. Write it upon our hearts so that we may become faithful actors in your unfolding drama. Amen.

Invite folks to the next session. Toss out a flavorful taste of the topic. Look ahead to prepare your supplies, plan, and publicity.

Session 2

Praying the Psalms
or, How to Use the Bible
to Improve Your Prayer Life

Matthew R. Schlimm

LEADER PREPARATION

Prepare Your Soul

Scripture

> Let us lift up our hearts as well as our hands to God in heaven.
> —Lamentations 3:41

Reflection

For some of us, prayer does not come easily. It can be difficult to find both the time and the words. Our thoughts easily get distracted and shift to other matters. A flood of ideas swamps our minds. We set out to pray, but before we even realize it, we've stopped praying and have focused on other things. Many of us feel we should turn to God more often, but maybe we don't know how to make it work.

One of the Bible's greatest gifts is its collection of 150 prayers, known as the Psalms. The Psalms give us words to pray when we have difficulty finding them. They equip us for lifting our hearts and minds — all that we are — to God. Here we find prayers for almost every occasion. From the depths of sorrow to the heights of jubilation, these prayers articulate ways to pray amid all sorts of experiences. In all seasons of life, they show us how we can be truly honest about ourselves before God.

When are the Psalms prayed in your church?

_____

_____

Have there been times in your life when you have used the Psalms in your personal devotional life? What about that experience went well? What was challenging?

_____

_____

What are your favorite Psalms? Why?

_____

_____

Prayer

> *Lord, teach us how to pray. Show me and the students how the Psalms can help us grow closer to you. Amen.*

Prepare Your Mind

The Psalms are one of the world's oldest collections of prayers. They were first prayed during worship in ancient Israel. Some Psalms date back to a thousand years before Christ. Since their composition, the Psalms have only increased in popularity. No other collection of prayers has been used by so many people in so many periods of history.

In both recent and ancient times, communities of faith have marked time by praying different types of Psalms. Certain Psalms were set aside for prayer in the morning and others for the evening. In seasons of sorrow, Lament Psalms were prayed. When ancient Israel crowned a new king, they prayed Royal Psalms. In times of harvest, Thanksgiving Psalms were prayed. In times of shock and anger, they prayed Psalms of Complaint. When the nation was at war, Psalms of Deliverance were prayed. Some Psalms were prayed corporately in worship; others were prayed individually.

Whereas much of the Bible is God's words to us, the Psalms are mostly our words to God. As inspired Scripture, they serve as models for shaping and forming our own prayer lives. Since ancient times, people have not only prayed the Psalms, but also created their own prayers using the Psalms as a guide. Archaeologists have found some prayers like this that date back to the time of Jesus.

The Bible's Psalms are prayers that were sung. In fact, over one-third of the Psalms begin with the words "For the choir director" (see "For the leader" in the NRSV). Likewise, the word *Selah* appears in a number of Psalms and is a musical term that appears to refer to a break or pause in the music. Other musical terms are found in the Psalms as well. Though we do not have the original tunes that ancient Israel sang with these songs, a number of churches continue the tradition of using music with Psalms and chant a different Psalm each Sunday.

Prepare Your Heart

Many of us have learned to pray with our eyes closed, our hands folded, and our heads bowed. We assume a certain posture. We talk a certain way. Usually, our prayers are polite. Emotions are often repressed. We don't usually scream out to God in prayer, point our fingers at God, or demand that God get to work — though some of us may. How do you pray? Do you feel safe expressing extreme emotion in prayer? Do the youth in your group express emotion in prayer?

Emotions are an essential part of who we are. We experience a range of them every day. With our emotions, we make sense of the world around us. When we sense that our world is threatening, we feel afraid, anxious, or worried. When we see that wonderful things have happened, we feel happiness and joy. When we encounter loss, sadness and grief well up within us. When we judge that the future holds bright things, we feel hope. What emotions have you experienced lately? What judgments accompany those feelings? What about the emotions of those in your group?

The Psalms are emotion-filled prayers. They show us how we can be honest about our feelings before God. When we feel joy, they allow us to thank God for the blessings we have received. When we feel threatened, they let us place our trust in God and learn that we are not alone. When we feel angry, they let us express our anger, even rage, so that we do not use it in destructive ways. What emotions do you (and those in your group) need help expressing to God?

Prepare Your Space

Arrange your space so that students can:

+ Face each other (preferably in a circle) for some parts of the lesson.
+ Face the television or screen for another part.
+ Operate independently of one another for a different part. You may want them to use other parts of the building or even go outside during this time. They will be praying during this time, so a chapel, garden, forest, or some other worshipful space would be appropriate.

Prepare Your Supplies

+ Television.
+ DVD or VCR Player.
+ Universal Studio's movie *The Apostle* (directed by and starring Robert Duvall).
+ Prepare by watching the clip. It begins 25 minutes, 33 seconds into the film. On some DVDs, this will be at the beginning of chapter 8. After a moment, this clip shows Sonny praying in his bedroom. Make sure the volume is loud enough to hear the woman who calls about 90 seconds into the clip. (On DVD players, you may want to show the English subtitles so everyone knows what is being said.) The clip ends at 27 minutes, 44 seconds (at the end of chapter 8 on some DVDs) when the film shows a car driving in the rain. When you see the car in the rain, stop the film and re-cue the movie so it is set for showing to participants (cue to 25:33, the beginning of chapter 8).
+ Bibles. One for each participant (or devise a plan for sharing), preferably in the same version (because they will be asked to pray Psalms in unison).

- Photocopies of the handouts found on pages 201–203. Participants should each have their own copy.

- Pencils or pens (markers or colored pencils could also be effective; participants will use these for writing prayers).

- Blank paper: several sheets for each participant, preferably without lines.

- Optional: Candles and matches or a lighter.

- Optional: Soothing instrumental music and a CD/MP3/cassette player.

Prepare Your Plan

This lesson allows students to be honest about their emotions with God by using the Psalms as their guide. It aims to teach them that they can prayerfully turn to God in all seasons of life.

Prepare Your Publicity

The following blurb could appear in a bulletin or newsletter: "Do you ever have trouble praying? If so, come to this week's workshop on 'Praying the Psalms,' where we will learn how the Psalms can guide us into a deeper life of prayer."

Prepare in Prayer

Gracious God, when you walked this earth, you made the deaf to hear, the mute to speak, and the blind to see. Open my ears to hear your word. Open my mouth to speak your word. Open my eyes to see you at work in my life and the lives of others.

I ask for clarity of thought as I teach. Help me to speak with passion in a way that others easily understand. I pray that you would especially help me as I . . .

_____

_____

_____

I pray for the hearts of our students. Send your comfort and peace as we bring our emotions to you. I pray for those who have emotional struggles in our group, especially for ...

———————————————————————————————————

———————————————————————————————————

———————————————————————————————————

I pray that our students would respect each other during our time together: that they would not demean or make fun of each other. Create a safe place among us. Help us to worship you. I pray for healing of tensions in our group between ...

———————————————————————————————————

———————————————————————————————————

———————————————————————————————————

We ask these things in your name. Amen.

Prepare Further

James L. Crenshaw, *The Psalms: An Introduction* (Eerdmans, 2001).
Walter Brueggemann, *The Message of the Psalms: A Theological Commentary* (Augsburg, 1984).

TEMPLATE FOR SESSION TWO
Praying the Psalms or, How to Use the Bible to Improve Your Prayer Life

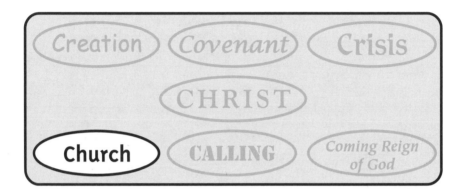

Key Scripture: Psalm 27:8

"Come," my heart says, "seek his face!" Your face, LORD, do I seek.

Objectives

- To learn more about the Psalms.
- To pray the Psalms.
- To use the Psalms as a guide for our own prayer lives.
- To become more comfortable bringing our emotions before God.

Welcome (2–5 minutes)

Greet participants and take care of announcements. Say something like, "I invite you to enjoy this time with God. To help your focus and that of your peers, please silence any potential distractions, including cell phones."

Lead participants in a prayer like the following (which is based in part on Psalm 139):

Loving God, you know everything about us.
You know when we sit down and when we stand up.
You know when we walk and when we rest.
You know all our ways, all our thoughts, all our words.
And yet, we often hide from you.
We often fail to come before you in prayer.
Help us to deepen our prayer life.
Lead us in the everlasting ways. Amen.

Tip: Why not invite a participant who arrives early to prepare to lead the opening prayer?

Invitation to Engagement:
Movie and Discussion (10–15 minutes)

Begin by saying that we will watch a clip from the movie *The Apostle.* Set up the movie by explaining the following:

* This movie tells the story of a charismatic preacher from Texas named Sonny.

* Sonny is a complex character. He is neither all good nor all bad.

* On the saintly side, he has a contagious faith, and he starts racially inclusive churches.

* On the sinful side, he is a womanizer, and he resorts to extreme violence to solve problems.

* In this clip, we see Sonny praying after his wife left him and he was fired as pastor of his church.

Play the clip, beginning 25 minutes, 33 seconds into the film. On some DVDs, this will be at the beginning of chapter 8. After a moment, it shows Sonny praying in his bedroom. Stop the movie after Sonny's mother finishes the phone conversation. The clip ends at 27 minutes, 44 seconds (at the end of chapter 8 on some DVDs) when the film shows a car driving in the rain.

Initiate a discussion of what the film portrays about emotions and prayer. The following questions can be used:

• What emotions did Sonny display?

• What actions accompanied these emotions?

• What did others (the neighbor, Sonny's mother) think of Sonny praying this way?

• We never see the neighbor praying. But if we did, what do you think her prayers might sound like? How might her prayers be different from Sonny's?

• Is your prayer life more like Sonny's or like the neighbor who called? Do you become angry and shout at God, or are you more reserved? Chat about this with someone near you, giving examples to illustrate your experiences of prayer.

• When you were a child, how were you taught to pray? What emotions were you taught to display in prayer? What were you taught to do with your hands, face, and voice while in prayer?

Discussion of Emotion in the Psalms (8–15 minutes)

Transition into a time of Bible study. Tell the students something like, "Surprisingly, many Psalms of the Bible sound more like Sonny than like the neighbor."

Have different students look up the following Scripture passages and hold them ready to read aloud in a few moments:

1. Psalm 13:1–2

2. Psalm 10:1

3. Psalm 44:23–24

4. Psalm 6:6–7

5. Psalm 102:9–11

Have them read aloud the first three examples (13:1–2, 10:1, 44:23–24). As they read, point out how the Psalmist seems angry with God, much like Sonny.

Next say something like, "The Psalms not only express anger, but also sadness and sorrow." Then have students read the remaining two passages (6:6–7; 102:9–11).

After these passages have been read, ask students something like, "Why do you think the Psalmists pray with such raw, negative emotion?"

Encourage discussion. Here are some possible responses you may want to explore:

* We all experience tragedy at different times in life. There's no need to pretend we're filled with joy when our world feels like it is crashing down around us.

* It is better to be honest than to be fake — especially with God.

* If we don't express our anger and grief, it can become corrosive inside us. As the saying goes, "Impression without expression leads to depression."

* It is better to speak angry words to God than to break off communication all together.

* God loves us, and we can be real with people who love us. God is our friend, and we can share our hearts with our friends.

* Time and again, God shows up in the midst of these prayers. Many Psalms begin with words of anger or sorrow, but then end with words of hope and comfort.

When discussion has drawn to a close, have students turn to Psalm 13 as a way of explaining how God often moves those who are praying from despair to hope. Say something like the following:

* "Psalm 13 is an example of a Psalm where the person praying starts off very angry. Let's read verses 1–2 together. . . . "

* "After voicing this anger to God, the person pleaded with God that God take action. Let's read verses 3–4 together. . . . "

* "Having voiced raw emotion to God and having asked for God's help, the person now places trust in God. Let's read verses 5–6 together. . . . "

- "God shows up in the midst of this person's anger and moves him or her to a better place. In the midst of prayer, the Psalmist finds a way to trust God again."

Ask students to keep their Bibles open to this Psalm.

Main Movement:
A Time to Pray the Psalms (20–40 minutes)

Instructions and Distributing the Handouts (5–10 minutes)

Say something like the following:

- The Psalms are a collection of prayers for all sorts of occasions. The ones we've looked at so far are for times of distress, anger, grief, and anguish.

- There are other types as well. Some Psalms are prayers for when we are happy and thankful. Others are for times when we want to say we're sorry for sins. Others are ones that can be prayed in the morning, afternoon, evening, or night.

- For thousands of years, people have used the Psalms as their guides in prayer. People often pray the Psalms as their own prayers. Other times, people read the Psalms and write their own prayers using the Psalms as their guide.

- What we're going to do now is to spend time individually praying the Psalms. I'd like you to spend a few minutes reflecting on the last week and what you are feeling. What went on in your family? at school? with your friends? How did that make you feel? *Hold up Handout 1 for chapter 2, found on page 201.*

- Then you will have time to pray some of the Psalms. I'm giving you a handout. (*Hold up the handout found on page 202.*) This handout organizes many of the Psalms into different categories. It lists ones that were prayed during anger, during happiness, during distress, as well as ones that were prayed in the morning, evening, and other times.

- I recognize that each of you is in a different place. Maybe some of you related to the angry prayers of Sonny and of Psalm 13.

Maybe others of you are feeling happy and didn't relate so well. Maybe others of you are feeling afraid about something in your lives. This handout can point you to different Psalms that may be appropriate for where you are today.

• I invite you to read three to five Psalms. Read each one slowly. Take a few moments to think about each Psalm before moving to the next one. As you read them, think about which one relates best to how you are feeling.

• Next, go back and reread your favorite Psalm, offering it to God as a prayer.

• After that, I invite you to write your own prayer. You may want to write a new prayer. Or you may want to add verses to one or more of the Psalms you read. Look back at Psalm 13, for example. In verses 1–2, the Psalmist asks, "How long?" several times. In the prayer you write, you may want to add your own "how long" questions. You may want to ask God, "How long will my parents keep fighting?" "How long will people make fun of me at school?" "How long will I hate the way I look?" Make the Psalms your own.

After these instructions, *distribute the handout on page 203,* pens and pencils, and blank paper. Tell the students how long they have to work on this exercise before gathering back as a group. Give options about spaces to which they might move in order to be one-on-one with God. Then dismiss them to go and pray using the Psalms.

Time Division for the Rest of the Main Movement
(25–50 minutes)

Time for students to find a place to go: 1–3 minutes.

Time with the handout: 13–25 minutes, including
Reflection: 3–5 minutes

Reading the Psalms: 5–10 minutes

Praying the Psalms: 5–10 minutes

Time for students to come back: 1–2 minutes

Reflection (5–10 minutes)

> If your group is smaller, discuss all together. If your group has more than eight participants, discuss in smaller groups of three or four people.

When the group reconvenes, discuss questions like the following:

• What was it like praying with the Psalms? Was it easy or difficult to use them? Why?

• Was there a Psalm or a verse that you especially liked? What did you like about it?

• Did you encounter a Psalm or a part of a Psalm that was difficult to pray? (If students answer yes, ask them to explain. You may want to tell them that not all Psalms fit every occasion in life.)

Worship (5–10 minutes)

For worship, you may want to play soft instrumental music, dim the lights, and light the candles.

Invite students to prayer, using words like the following: "We are going to close with a time of prayer. We each will have a chance to pray. We will go around in a circle. You can pray using a verse or more from the Psalms or from a prayer you wrote. If you don't feel comfortable praying aloud, you can say 'Lord, hear our prayer' or 'pass.'"

After giving students time to find a verse (or more), begin with a brief prayer of your own.

After each student has prayed, conclude the prayer. Here is a prayer that could be used:

Gracious God, help us to see you as our friend. Help us to share our hearts with you in all periods of life. Thank you that no matter what we face, we can be honest and open with you. Amen.

Alternative Ideas for Worship

+ Instead of having each student pray part of a prayer, you may want everyone to pray a Psalm together. The leader could read the odd-numbered verses, for example, and the students could read the even-numbered verses.

+ Alternatively, if your church has hymnals that include Psalms marked for chanting or singing, you could lead the youth in singing a Psalm.

+ Another alternative is to pray Psalm 136 together. Students can take turns reading the beginning of each verse, and then everyone can read together the response, such as "for his steadfast love endures forever."

Follow-up and Announcements

Encourage students to hold on to the handout and use the Psalms as a guide for prayer. Remind them that they can turn to God with whatever they are feeling.

Before dismissing them, you may want to offer a chance for individuals to talk with you one-on-one in case they need to discuss any emotions they are experiencing.

Here are some ideas for follow-up:

+ Meet with students for Morning, Noonday, Evening, or Nighttime (Compline) Prayer. These prayer services are usually brief (about 15–30 minutes) and include a number of Psalms. Many pastors have resources for leading such services, as do some hymnals.

+ Start a "Praying the Psalms" group where a different type of Psalm is studied each week.

+ Arrange for the students to lead the congregation in praying a Psalm during Sunday morning worship.

Session 3

The Word Made Flesh: Embodying and Telling the Stories of the Bible

Tracy Radosevic

LEADER PREPARATION

Prepare Your Soul

"I will open my mouth in a story...." (Psalm 78:2, translation by Radosevic's colleagues in Network of Biblical Storytellers, from the website *http://nbsint.org/festgath.html*).

There are all kinds of stories, including family stories, adventure stories, fish stories, heartfelt stories, heartbreak stories, sob stories, triumph stories, amazing stories, children's stories, inspirational stories, and teaching stories.

Who do you know who can tell a good story?

_____

_____

_____

What makes for a good telling?

_____

_____

_____

Do you tend to be more intrigued by the details or the concepts of a story?

_____

_____

_____

With whom can you easily identify in a story? Why?

_____

_____

_____

Read Matthew 3:13–17. In a moment of quiet reflection, let God bring a biblical story to your soulful awareness. What grabs your attention in this story?

_____

_____

_____

With whom can you identify or sympathize?

_____

_____

_____

What truth does this story contain for you?

_____

_____

_____

Jot down three words you might use in telling the story of what God is up to in your life these days.

_____

_____

_____

Who could you tell?

_____

_____

Prepare Your Mind

Recitation of Scripture is one of the most consistent actions performed by churches across denominational lines. We do it in worship, in Sunday school class, with our youth group, and of course as the key element of a Bible study session. This activity has strong precedents, firmly grounded in our Jewish roots. The *Shema* (Deuteronomy 6:4–9), the core Hebrew prayer that affirms the monotheism of God and how we're to relate to that one God, also contains clear instructions for how to remember — and pass on — this essential belief: "Keep these words that I am commanding you today *in your heart. Recite them* to your children and *talk about them* when you are at home and when you are away, when you lie down and when you rise." In Hebrew physiology, the locus for memory was not in the head but in the heart. The implication here is that our sacred texts need to enter deeply into the core of our being, where we not only hear them but truly *experience* them — sometimes in a visceral way — and where they can interact with our emotions, our will, our actions.

Many people, if asked, could recite the formula Albert Einstein is perhaps most famous for: $E=MC^2$. Most of those same people, however, have no real understanding of what that formula really means, nor would they be able to explain it in an easily comprehendible way to a novice. It's one thing to know something *in your head* and to be able to recite it from memory, but it's something else entirely to know, *in your heart,* what it actually means (and, in the case of the Bible, to then live out in your life what it implies, intends, and calls for).

Similarly, many Christians can recite John 3:16 — "For God so loved the world that he gave his only Son, so that everyone who believes in him may not perish but may have eternal life" — and that's great! But what does it really mean, in a practical, everyday-living kind of way? What it has often led to is a rigid tendency toward condemning and threatening those who *don't* believe in the Son with an eternity of hellfire and damnation. Many of those same reciters, however, have no idea how this passage continues, for the very next verse, John 3:17 says, "Indeed, God did not send the Son into the world to condemn the world, but in order that the world might be saved through him." This is a much more graceful, compassionate, and encouraging approach to evangelism. Again, it's one thing to know the words; it's another to understand them.

Knowing the right thing to do — but not necessarily doing it — is kind of like the lawyer (an expert in "right and wrong," by the way!) in Luke 10:25–28 who asks Jesus what he must do to inherit eternal life. It turns out he actually knows the answer, rattling off Deuteronomy 6:5 in short order. But he apparently doesn't fully understand what that means because he presses Jesus to further explain, resulting in Jesus telling the parable of the Good Samaritan. The whole exchange ends with Jesus telling him to "go and *do* likewise" (Luke 10:37).

One of the best ways to put our thoughts and knowledge into action is to initially learn, and then store, information in an experiential way that involves more than just our heads or minds. The more members of the body that are utilized in internalization, the more members there will subsequently be to call upon to truly *re-member* that information later. If a story, for instance, has been embodied, using not only the heart and gut but the arms, hands, fingers, legs, feet, toes, eyes, eyebrows, lips, etc., then parts of the story seem to actually get stored in those various body parts. This tremendously helps the brain, which then doesn't have to work all by itself when later trying to recall the story. And more than just a practical aid, it's also theological because this embodiment echoes elements of incarnation. A biblical story that has been deeply dived into paradoxically resides more deeply within the learner. Any eventual telling then literally comes from the core being of the teller in such a way that the lifeless text from the lifeless page of a book can truly be experienced as the *Living Word*. It's our opportunity to enter into a new creation of the Word becoming flesh.

Prepare Your Heart

As Christians, we know that the Bible is important, sacred, and deserving of our respect. The problem is that it has so frequently been presented in a dry, dull, difficult-to-understand way that it's often difficult to drum up any interest or enthusiasm for hearing it, let alone studying it. For many, the reading of Scripture is when people "check out" — their minds begin to wander and it's when they are the least engaged. Someone might wonder, "The Bible is significant, yes, but is it really relevant? I mean, these are stories that happened to people a *long* time ago in a land far, far away. It was a completely different culture. Times have changed. So does the Bible really have anything to say to me? Anything that pertains to my life and the issues I'm currently dealing with?"

Yes!

A strong argument could be made that no modern-day movie, TV show, or song (not to mention real-life, personal experience) has anything on the Bible. It's got it all! Sibling rivalry, mixed families, deceit, miscommunication, raging hormones, betrayal, peer pressure, poor decisions, illness, poverty, power struggles, war, isolation, desperation, struggles with faith and vocational discernment, as well as love, compassion, forgiveness, hospitality, community, understanding, peace, faith, and truth (just to name a few). More important, all these stories are anchored by and connected to God who is most certainly relevant to our lives today!

So what's the best way to prepare our hearts to welcome — and actually *experience* — these relevant stories of God? Maybe by realizing, first of all, that the biblical texts were never meant to be read in silence. They were meant to be performed, just like a score of music.

Can you imagine a large crowd gathering in a concert hall, being given the printed score to Beethoven's Ninth Symphony, and then everyone sitting in silence studying it, perhaps followed by someone getting up and lecturing *about* the score? Actually, can you imagine even an individual music student experiencing Beethoven's Ninth Symphony *only* in this way? Of course not; that would be ridiculous. And yet, isn't that exactly what we've done for several hundred years with the Bible?

The word "performed" is intentionally used because it implies that the "performer" has spent time with the text, knows it well, and presents it in an audible way that involves a certain level of competence. At the very least, it means that all words are pronounced correctly and confidently. But it also presupposes that some feeling, inflections, pauses, and maybe even a gesture and "look" or two are employed in the presentation as well. Of course, this requires that time be set aside for preparation. You can't expect much if you recruit people at the last minute to read Scripture. They should be given plenty of time to digest the passage. It's best if they can live with it for a time so as to feel comfortable and familiar with it. They need time in order to have made some personal connections with it. Ideally, when these elements are recognized and implemented, then any subsequent performance of the text will most assuredly be more engaging, interesting, and relevant. So the best way for you to prepare your heart is to start familiarizing yourself with this session's story well in advance of its presentation.

Tip: Dr. Radosevic, a veteran storyteller, recommends familiarizing yourself with a biblical story a month beforehand, so there will be adequate time to live with it.

Prepare Your Space

The venue should be as bright and spacious as possible, allowing for all participants to move about, and see, unimpeded. Tape one of the four pictures symbolizing a method for baptism (see supplies below) to each of the four walls. Put a circle of chairs in front of each picture (ideally you'd have close to an even four-way split of how each of your youth were baptized. This probably isn't likely, however, with a majority of them being baptized via the method most frequently used in your congregation or tradition. So more chairs should be placed in front of that picture, with the option of further subdividing that group later.) Finally, place a stool or small table near the entrance to the room. This is where the bowl of water will go once the session begins.

Prepare Your Supplies

• A bowl of water (on a stool or small table).

• A picture of drops of water, with the word "sprinkle" displayed prominently on it.

• A picture of water pouring from a pitcher, with the word "pour" displayed prominently on it.

• A picture of a baptistery or a large baptismal font for immersion, with the word "immersed" displayed prominently on it.

• A picture of a river or lake, with the word "natural" displayed prominently on it.

• Tape.

• Water/baptism-related songs and some sort of music player.

• A copy of the Matthew 3:13–17 handout for each person (see below page 204).

• A pencil or pen for each participant.

• Bible: Well before the session, mark 2 Corinthians 5:16–20 and recruit a volunteer to read it.

Prepare Your Plan

This session will explore different ways to internalize a biblical story in a truly embodied/incarnate way, culminating in the telling of that story in small groups or to the whole group, if desired. A secondary goal is for participants to think about the experience of their own baptisms, to explore what being baptized really means, and to make connections between their baptism and Jesus' baptism. You, as the leader, need to have gone through the process first so that you are comfortable with the story, know it well, and have made personal connections with it, including any kind of correspondence between it and your baptismal experience.

Prepare Your Publicity

Conventional wisdom states that, if it's at all possible, it's better to show than to tell. You can talk *about* storytelling until you're blue in the face, but it's a pale substitute for experiencing it. So telling a story, or a piece of it, at the previous week's youth fellowship gathering, or in worship, would be ideal. A portion of the told story could also be videotaped and posted on the church website, on Facebook, or sent out with an e-mail invitation. What really might get people's attention is something like: "Come for an evening full of B.S. (meaning *biblical storytelling*, of course!)"

Prepare in Prayer

God of Story, thank you for the written account of your gracious activity in the world throughout the ages and among generations of our forebears. Your embodied presence, through the life and person of Jesus and the stories we have of his ministry, are an inspiration to us today. Help us to more fully experience the incarnate aspect of faith and life by digging deeply into this particular Bible story and allowing it to take residence within us. Help us, then, to enable the youth of this church to do the same so that we may all draw closer to you, understand you better, and gain a clearer path for our faith journey together. Amen.

Prepare Further

You might find it helpful to look at chapter 4 of Fred Edie's *Book, Bath, Table, and Time,* particularly pages 108–10 and 117–25.

Other great resources are Thomas Boomershine's *Story Journey: An Invitation to the Gospel as Storytelling* (Abingdon, 1988) as well as the websites for the Network of Biblical Storytellers (*http://nbsint.org/*) and Go Tell Communications, especially the page dealing with our chosen story (*http://gotell.org/pages/stories/Matthew/Mt03_13-17.html*).

TEMPLATE FOR SESSION THREE
The Word Made Flesh:
Embodying and Telling the Stories of the Bible

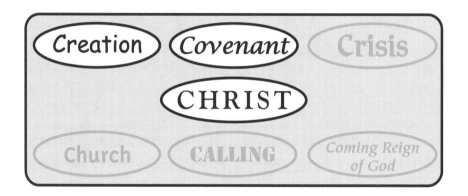

Key Scripture: Matthew 3:13

Then Jesus came from Galilee to John at the Jordan, to be baptized by him.

Objectives

- For the participants to remember their baptism (or think about what they might like their baptism experience to be).
- To experience a live telling of the embodied story of Jesus' baptism from Matthew 3:13–17.
- To explore personal connections with this story.
- To internalize this story through a variety of embodying methods.
- To tell this story (to a small group and possibly to the whole group).

Welcome (7–12 minutes)

As the participants arrive, stand next to the bowl of water at the entrance to the room. Warmly greet them and invite them to touch

40

the water and "get wet" in some way (without making a big mess!). Point out the four pictures hanging on the walls and instruct them to go sit in front of the one that depicts most closely how they were baptized. (If they haven't been baptized yet, ask them to sit in front of the method that they would most like to have used if and when they're baptized.) Tell them to meditate on the picture while remembering their baptism, stories they've heard about their baptism, or baptisms they've witnessed. Once others join, form a circle near each picture. Invite participants to share these stories, observations, and experiences with each other. (It might help to facilitate this process if there is an adult or youth leader stationed at each circle.) You may also want to have water sounds or baptism-related music playing, particularly before a critical mass gathers.

Prayer (1–2 minutes)

Cleansing God, through baptism we are made new, re-created, and connected with the many water stories of renewal in the Bible. Be with us now as we create something new within ourselves and our community by diving into the story of Jesus' baptism. Amen.

Invitation to Engagement (7–10 minutes)

Summarize for participants the information from the "Prepare Your Mind" preparatory section (page 34).

Tell the story of Jesus' baptism from Matthew 3:13–17. Ask:

• What did you notice?

• Are there any elements from this story that you remember from other Bible stories?

• Are there any connections between Jesus' baptism and your baptism? Like what?

Main Movement: Storytelling (25–35 minutes)

Hand out the Matthew 3 narrative to everyone. The handout can be found on page 204.

Say something like, "The words on the handout come straight from the Bible (Matthew 3:13–17), but the look here is somewhat different. Can you name the differences?"

- The verse numbers have been removed. They serve no purpose in a performed story and can potentially slow down the flow of the narrative.

- The story has been divided into three episodes. Episodes are like paragraphs, a new one starting each time the action changes.

- This version has weird indentations. Each new sentence starts out at the far left margin and continues on that line until a new thought-phrase, which goes on the next line down, indented once. This format continues with each new thought-phrase on its own indented line until the end of the sentence. This is to more easily facilitate the memory of the story, making it clear, at a glance, how many sentences each episode has: in this case, two.

Hand out a pencil or pen to the participants while they silently read their handout.

Do you think it was *necessary* for Jesus to be baptized? Why or why not? What do you think Jesus meant when he said to John, "It is proper for us in this way to fulfill all righteousness"?

Have each participant pick one word that best summarizes what each episode is about and write those words next to the episode each is representing, over at the far right-hand side of the paper.

Have them get with a partner from their small group and, after folding their handout so that only their three words are visible, tell their partner about what's going on in each episode, using their chosen words to trigger their memory. (*Note:* Tell the participants that it's okay to be a little vague at this point. Try to remember, but don't stress over details!) Then switch roles. After each is done, they should check to see what major details they left out. Also, if any of the three summarizing words they chose weren't as helpful as they would have liked, have them choose a new word.

Have the youth underline all the action words in the narrative.

Then have them turn over their papers and on the back illustrate the action of the story. There are at least three possible ways to do this (and make it clear that stick figures are fine!):

1. One picture that depicts the entire story (like da Vinci's *Last Supper* painting)

2. A storyboard (like cartoon strips) that depict the varied actions of the story. (I'd suggest at least six separate drawings here, one for each sentence.)

3. A bird's-eye view of the stage, where the location for each of the characters and props are all drawn in. (If there's movement, like when Jesus initially comes from Galilee to the Jordan River, then indicate — perhaps with a "J" for Jesus in two different spots and an arrow connecting them — that movement for Jesus has occurred.)

Now have the participants take turns "acting out" the story to a group of three or four others, using their illustrations as an aid. Encourage them to pay attention to the physical cues in the story and to embody them in their tellings (e.g., How did Jesus "come out of" the water? Had John bent him backward? Forward? Straight down — which would imply that Jesus had to bend his knees and kneel? What could you do with your body as a storyteller when you get to the parts that say the "heavens were opened to him" and "the Spirit of God descending like a dove and alighting on him"?) The listeners should *not* be reading along but should be fully attentive to the teller, with their papers put aside. The tellers can use their drawings as an aid. After each telling, all in the group should check to see what details were left out. Each should try to be more precise this go around than when they told the story to a partner the first time.

Finally, invite each small group to tell the story among themselves communally. Everyone should put down their papers and face each other in the circle. One person starts out the story, saying only a phrase. Another person, who thinks they know what comes next, should say the next phrase. This continues until the whole story gets told by the group. If at any time during the story someone inadvertently leaves out a piece, the person who realizes this should gently interrupt by saying, "But before that happened..." and fill in the missing piece of the story. Afterward everyone can check to see if anything was left out.

Now invite each person to tell the entire story to their small group without the help of their paper. They should be encouraged to visualize the story as clearly as possible within themselves and to then try to get their group to see what they're seeing by using facial expressions, hand gestures, different postures and body elevations, movement, etc. Once everyone has had an opportunity to try it, have the participants discuss what they noticed in the different tellings.

> The words matter. Many people think they can't trust the stories "as is" because they aren't interesting enough to hold anyone's attention; they think that the story needs to be "jazzed up" by putting it in our own words. There is a time and place for creative midrash, but for this exercise encourage the participants to stick close to the "script," aiming for at least 75 percent word accuracy and 95 percent content accuracy.

Reflection: Life-Swim (10–15 minutes)

Hand out the preprinted journaling questions to each participant and invite them to find a quiet place in the room to settle down, meditate, and "journal" (this can include drawings) about the questions listed in the handout on page 205.

Worship (10–15 minutes)

Bring the bowl of water and its stand into the center of the room. Gather everyone in a circle around it. Ask for a volunteer to tell the

This session is just the beginning of the
experience. The story will continue to
grow within and speak to each participant,
particularly if future activities are employed to
encourage ongoing exploration and connection-
making with it. Maybe this could be facilitated
each week by having the bowl of water available
for "getting wet" either as the youth enter or
leave. Teaching them to say, "I remember my
baptism and am thankful," or having someone
say to them, "Remember your baptism and
be thankful," as they get wet is also a good
practice. In fact, they could be encouraged
to not only remember *their* baptism, but the
story of Jesus' baptism — even telling it quickly
to themselves — every time they "get wet"
(bathing, in the rain, swimming, washing their
hands, etc.)

baptism of Jesus story from Matthew 3. Afterward invite everyone, in silence, to think about their own baptism, especially in relation to Jesus' baptism. Have a volunteer read 2 Corinthians 5:16–20. Say: "The phrase 'in Christ' could be considered code for 'baptized.' So this passage suggests that our baptism connects us to God in a reconciling way. The old, or things of the past, are gone, washed away, and we're made new. This is good news...but easy to forget sometimes." Invite the youth to come to the water bowl/baptismal font when they feel ready. When the first youth comes forward, the leader wets her or his own fingers in the water and makes the sign of the cross on the youth's forehead saying, "Remember your baptism and be thankful." Then invite that youth to do the same thing for the next person who comes forward. That person then performs the ritual for the third and so on until everyone who wishes to come forward has done so (the last person makes the sign of the cross on the initial leader's forehead).

Benediction

> *We are ambassadors for Christ. So go into the world this week remembering who and whose you are and living your life as a new creation, reconciled to God. Amen.*

The coming forward during worship is an invitation only; participants shouldn't feel obligated to do this, especially if they haven't been baptized. If there is just one person who has not been baptized, he or she could hold the bowl of water and walk around the circle while the other participants bless each other with the water. Another way to be sure to include those who have not been baptized is to ask them to be the teller and Scripture reader.

Follow-up and Announcements

Remind the group that tonight's experience just planted the seed; the story will continue to grow within them in wonderful, and perhaps surprising, ways. But, as with any plant, it needs to be nourished. So encourage the group to continue to tell the Matthew 3 baptism story throughout the week, preferably every day (perhaps as a morning or evening devotional), paying attention to any other parts or aspects of the story that seem to be nudging, bothering, or inspiring them. Even better, see if they can find at least three people to tell the story to the group that week, paying attention to what insights they glean from these different audiences. Journal all comments, observations, insights.

What Next?

What story could be told next in your group? Consider Matthew 4:18–22 (Jesus calls) and Matthew 3:1–12 (John baptizes).

Session 4

Echoes of Jesus: Old Testament Anticipations of the Coming Messiah

Andrew C. Thompson

LEADER PREPARATION

Prepare Your Soul

Behold, the virgin shall conceive and bear a Son, and shall call His name Immanuel. — Isaiah 7:14, NKJV

When I was a child, we celebrated Christmas at my grandparents' house in Jonesboro, Arkansas. Our Christmas day tradition was always the same. We arrived early in the morning in anticipation of a huge Christmas dinner. We feasted at noon, with the sounds of laughter and conversation reminding all of us how good it was to be with family on that special day.

After the plates were cleared away but before we exchanged gifts, we had our annual Christmas pageant. This was our family's way of entering into the story of Jesus' birth, taught to us by my grandmother and my mom. For a little while on Christmas afternoon, my grandparents' living room would be transformed into Bethlehem. And we all became the biblical characters from the Nativity story — grandparents and parents, aunts and uncles, and kids took on the roles of Mary and Joseph, shepherds and wise men, angels and innkeepers. As the number of kids in the family grew over the years, we even added parts — like the "innkeeper's son" — just to make sure that everybody got a part. And we made the story more real by dressing up in robes and turbans and crowns, with walking staffs for the shepherds and little jewelry boxes for the wise men's gold, frankincense, and myrrh.

One of the adults served as the Christmas pageant narrator, reading mostly from the Gospels of Matthew and Luke in the New Testament. But we always started and ended in the Old Testament, with certain passages from the prophet Isaiah. Our little pageant began with Isaiah 7:14, which says, "Behold, the virgin shall conceive and bear a Son, and shall call His name Immanuel" (NKJV). And after we went through the drama of Mary and Joseph's journey to Bethlehem and the birth of the baby Jesus, we ended with Isaiah 9:6–7:

> For unto us a Child is born,
> unto us a Son is given;
> and the government will be upon His shoulder.
> And His name will be called
> Wonderful, Counselor, Mighty God,
> Everlasting Father, Prince of Peace.
> Of the increase of His government and peace
> there will be no end,
> upon the throne of David and over His kingdom
> to order it and establish it with judgment and justice
> from that time forward, even forever.
> The zeal of the LORD of hosts will perform this. (NKJV)

Perhaps you've heard those passages from Isaiah during Advent in your own church. In fact, you might associate them automatically with the coming of Jesus. But have you ever thought about how far away they are — both in time and in their place in the Bible — from the New Testament? Isaiah, the son of Amoz, lived seven hundred years before Jesus' birth! And the book of the Bible that bears his name comes after the Song of Solomon and before Jeremiah; in other words, it is nowhere near the four Gospels (Matthew, Mark, Luke, and John) that tell us about Jesus' life.

So why do we assume that Isaiah said something that relates directly to Jesus? The answer to that question has to do with the way that Christians believe Jesus stands at the center of the great story of God and God's people.

> Why do we assume that Isaiah said something
> that relates directly to Jesus, born hundreds of
> years later?

The actual accounts of Jesus' birth and infancy are found in two places in the New Testament: Matthew 1:18–2:23 and Luke 1:5–2:20. But since the earliest Christian times, the church has seen the coming of Jesus as *foretold* through Old Testament prophecy. In fact, Isaiah 7:14 ("the virgin shall conceive and bear a Son") is mentioned explicitly in Matthew 1:23 in connecting Jesus' birth with the fulfillment of the prophet's message. And while Isaiah's prophecy about Jesus is perhaps the best known, there are many other stories and images from the Hebrew Scriptures that prefigure Jesus' life, ministry, and death. So to understand why Christians believe that the entire Bible (from Genesis to Revelation!) is sacred, we need to focus on Jesus and how he fits into the story of God's people Israel. Doing that can open the Scriptures up to us in a whole new way, much like they were opened up to me as a child when my family performed the Christmas pageant each year.

• When do you read from the Old Testament? Is it often or rare?

_____

_____

_____

• What Old Testament stories are important to you?

_____

_____

_____

• How did you come to know the stories of Jesus?

_____

_____

_____

Prepare Your Mind

To understand how the Old and New Testaments relate to one another, we turn to one of our "Alliterative C's." This time we look at *Christ,* which is a word that means *Messiah*. In Jewish understanding, the Messiah is the anointed one of God sent to liberate and lead God's people Israel. The good news of Jesus is that *he* is the Christ, the Messiah who has been sent to set God's people free from all that binds them. Jesus himself tells us that his mission is not to overturn all of God the Father's story with Israel as told in the Torah and the prophets, but rather to bring it to a climax: "Do not think that I have come to abolish the law or the prophets," Jesus preaches in the Sermon on the Mount, "I have come not to abolish but to fulfill" (Matthew 5:17).

One of the most important things for youth and adults to understand when they approach the Bible is that Christians regard *both* the Old and New Testaments as God's word to us. So "old" in reference to the Old Testament doesn't mean "outdated"! We divide the Bible into two different testaments for a number of reasons, but the most important is the one we find explained in Hebrews 1:1–2: "Long ago God spoke to our ancestors in many and various ways by the prophets, but in these last days he has spoken to us by a Son, whom he appointed heir of all things, through whom he also created the worlds." So the Old Testament is "old" only because it tells about the "long ago," through the story of God and God's people — Israel — before the Incarnation of God in the person of Jesus. And the New Testament is "new" in that it shows us the way that the good news of Jesus has "broken down the dividing wall" (Ephesians 2:14) between Jew and Gentile and called all nations to be incorporated into God's family. And it is also "new" in that Jesus himself — through his life, death, and resurrection — has opened the way to full salvation by reconciling the world to God's own self. And so, through Jesus, there is a new expression of what it means to be a part of the people of God: what we call the *church*.

But the Old Testament remains as important as it ever was! And in fact, from the time of the apostles' ministry, Christians have seen ways that the Old Testament Scriptures connect with Jesus by *prefiguring*

> Ever wonder why the Old Testament is "old" and
> the New Testament is "new"?

his coming into the world. That is, when we read the Old Testament through our knowledge of Jesus Christ, we can see how God was preparing the way for the Incarnation by the revelation of his word to Israel. Time and again, we can see echoes of Jesus sounding through the story of Noah and the Flood, the story of Moses and the Exodus, and the ministry of prophets like Isaiah and Malachi.

The technical name for these prefiguring images of the Messiah — these *echoes of Jesus* — is *typology*. It's not so important to teach that term to your students, but it is important for you as the leader to know what it means. It refers to the way that we see "types" or "prefigurations" of Jesus' life and ministry in certain important Old Testament stories and images. Another way to think about this (and one that might work better with youth) is that we find Jesus himself specifically *anticipated* in some of Israel's most dramatic moments, hundreds of years before Jesus' own birth.

> "Typology" is a way of reading the Bible that
> focuses on how stories and images in the Old
> Testament anticipate or prefigure the coming of
> Jesus as Savior of the world.

Some might ask the question, "If we can just go to the New Testament and find out about Jesus directly, why should we even bother with searching through the Old Testament for hints of him there?" Well, those words from Jesus quoted above, about coming to *fulfill* the law and the prophets, are a good place to start. God the Father did not open up heaven and send Jesus the Son down on a whim. God had been in relationship with Israel since the time Abraham and Sarah were called out of Haran to go to the land of Canaan (Genesis 12). And in all that time, God had been working to repair the damage that had been done to humanity since the Fall of Adam and Eve (Genesis 3). God called the people into a covenant relationship, gave them the law through Moses and repeatedly called them back to faithfulness through the ministry of the prophets when they went astray. And all that time, God was preparing the way so that he could enter history directly in the person of Jesus Christ.

Put simply, *the story matters*. We can't fully know who Jesus is without first knowing about the relationship of God and Israel. And when the apostles began recording the words that would become the books of the New Testament, they believed the story mattered, too. In *Book, Bath, Table, and Time,* Fred Edie explains that "the New Testament writers worked from the assumption that Jesus as messiah was the central antitype pointed to by many other Old Testament persons and events, which therefore were considered 'types' or 'prefigurements' of Jesus" (p. 114). The inspired writers of the New Testament saw their own times as shaped by the history that preceded them. And the same is true for us as well when we look back into the Old Testament for echoes of Jesus. Edie adds, "Typology provides the means to read the Scriptures as unfolding story and therefore supports the formation of communal identity around this story" (p. 115). The Scriptures — from both testaments — shape and form us as we understand Jesus' central role in them and our place as those who carry on the story that they tell.

So what are these stories from the Bible that prefigure the coming of Jesus even back in the time of the Old Testament? We will focus on passages from the Old Testament that the New Testament itself points toward as anticipating Jesus. For instance, think of the stories about Noah and the Great Flood, the Hebrews' escape after God "passed over" their children in the dreadful final plague against Egypt, and the trials that Moses and the Israelites faced during their time in the wilderness. These are all dramatic episodes in the great story of God and God's people. But the New Testament also sees Jesus in each of them as they prefigure how he would come to renew the covenant and restore the creation.

Prepare Your Heart

• How familiar are you with the Bible? Is your relationship with the Bible more like an acquaintance or a familiar friend? Like a grandparent or a distant cousin?

• How familiar are your students with the Bible? What's that relationship like?

We often hear about the decline of "biblical literacy" in our culture and in our churches. And it's true that the explosion of print and electronic media has meant that we have an almost limitless amount of books, TV shows, websites, magazines, and blogs to read or watch. Even for committed disciples in the church, we may no longer be able to assume a basic familiarity with the Bible.

The good news is that young people seem to be as interested in Jesus as ever! His proclamation of good news, his call to repent, and his offer of life abundant continue to touch all people, young and old, at the deepest part of their souls. And because of that, we can expect our youth to be gripped by the stories of Jesus in the Gospels, if we will but place them at the heart of our teaching and ministry.

> **Young people seem to be as interested in Jesus as ever!**

But what about the rest of the Bible, the parts where Jesus doesn't directly appear?

The majority of the Scriptures, for instance, fall within the bounds of the Old Testament. The thirty-nine Old Testament books really make up a small library of holy literature, consisting of history, genealogy, wisdom sayings, poetry, and prophecy. To the unfamiliar, it can seem rather daunting! And so one way that we — and especially our youth — can begin to have the word of God written upon our hearts is through focusing on those parts of Holy Scripture in the Old Testament where we find echoes of Jesus, our Savior, anticipated through the story of God's people Israel.

The beauty of the Scriptures is that we can learn them in so many ways. We learn from the Bible every time we hear a sermon. Some of the best Christian music lyrics — from traditional hymns to contemporary praise songs — are basically just Bible passages turned into song. And of course, a daily devotional is another wonderful way to commit God's word to your heart. So think of this lesson, where we are learning to connect the Old and New Testaments through Jesus, as another way to receive God's grace through the study of Scripture.

Prepare Your Space

It will be best to divide your youth into three more-or-less equal groups. Appoint a leader for each group. When a youth is the leader it would still be good to have adults for each group. Have each of the three groups sit in a circle, either in chairs or on the floor. They will also need Bibles so they can take turns reading and follow along with the stories that are being shared. Ideally, the groups could also be spaced far enough apart (or in different rooms) so that they can engage in conversation without distracting one another.

If your church has stained-glass windows, there will be an optional exercise at the end to search for biblical images in the stained glass. You will need to make sure the sanctuary, chapel, narthex/foyer, or other parts of the church with stained-glass windows are available to you. If your church does not have stained-glass windows but you know of a nearby church that does, you might consider arranging to have your youth group visit that church either on the day of this lesson or at another appropriate time.

Prepare Your Supplies

Each participant will need access to a Bible. (It will help if everyone uses the same translation, although that is not absolutely necessary.) Also provide blank sheets of paper and pencils or pens for an introductory writing exercise, as well as for notes if any of your youth want to write down things to remember. Have the questions for the opener written for all to see.

You will also be breaking your total group up into three smaller groups with a leader for each of the smaller groups. So it will be important for your adults and volunteer leaders to have access to the session itself so they can read the assigned biblical passages and relevant aids ahead of time. Because of "Bible study" nature of this particular session, that kind of advance reading on the part of your adult volunteers will be very helpful. So please, give them a heads-up and a handout ahead of time.

- Have handouts ready for group leaders.
- Have copies of Advancing Echoes (page 209), if needed, either for an advanced group or for take-home. If the closing time of worship will include Eucharist/Holy Communion, plan for needed elements and officiants.

Prepare Your Plan

This session will help youth begin to make connections between the Old and New Testaments. It will help to spark an interest in the deep theological meaning connected to many of the most important Old Testament stories. Most important, this session will help your youth see how Jesus Christ is at the center of God's story with God's people, in that, ultimately, all of Scripture points to the Incarnation of God in Christ Jesus our Lord! This session will invite participants to think of the Bible as a great unfolding story and to view their own discipleship as a connected part of the same story, by emphasizing that we are a part of the same church that God first calls together in Scripture.

Jesus Christ is at the center of God's story.

Prepare Your Publicity

How do you communicate with your youth? Do you have a regularly updated website? An e-mail list? A regular newsletter that gets mailed out? Consider announcing this session by asking the question, "Where do we find Jesus in the Old Testament?" You might offer a prize (e.g., candy, gift certificate) for the participant who comes up with the most convincing answer.

Prepare in Prayer

Holy God, you have called your people to be in covenant relationship with you. You rescued Noah and his family from the Flood. You raised up Moses and the Hebrews out of Egypt. And you provided for your people in the wilderness by giving them manna from heaven and water from the rock. These miraculous events are a part of your story with us, and they all prefigured the greatest miracle of all — your Incarnation into the world through Jesus Christ. Thank you for the wonders of your holy word in the Scriptures; let us receive that word into our very hearts. Mold us into your people, that we might receive the fullness of your salvation. We offer praise and thanksgiving in the name of Jesus Christ. Amen.

Prepare Further

There are a number of good resources that you can consult to fill out your understanding of typological readings of the Bible. Here are two that would be particularly helpful for the interested youth minister or volunteer youth worker:

Fred Edie, "The Book Becomes Script: Youth Practice Storied Performances of the Bible," chapter 4, in *Book, Bath, Table, and Time: Christian Worship as Source and Resource for Youth Ministry* (Pilgrim Press, 2007), 93–125. This chapter has a very helpful section on reading the Bible typologically. Dr. Edie points out that a typological reading of the Old Testament (contrary to some critiques of that approach) actually invites Christians to take the Old Testament seriously as part of God's word that is intimately connected with Jesus Christ. He also explains how seeing Old Testament stories and symbols as prefigurements of Christ and the church can help us to read the whole Bible as God's unfolding story of covenant with God's people — an approach that can bear fruit in helping youth to gain familiarity (and fascination!) with the Scriptures.

G. K. Beale and D. A. Carson, eds., *Commentary on the New Testament Use of the Old Testament* (Baker Academic Press, 2007). This commentary (of over twelve hundred pages) has chapters covering every book of the New Testament.

Ben Witherington, III. *Making a Meal of It: Rethinking the Theology of the Lord's Supper* (Baylor University Press, 2007). Dr. Witherington's book is aimed at a lay reading audience and is designed to help the reader better understand the meaning and significance of the Lord's Supper. Dr. Witherington ably takes the reader through the various connections between the Hebrew practice of Passover in the Old Testament and the Christian practice of Holy Communion in the New Testament.

TEMPLATE FOR SESSION FOUR
Echoes of Jesus: Old Testament Anticipations of the Coming Messiah

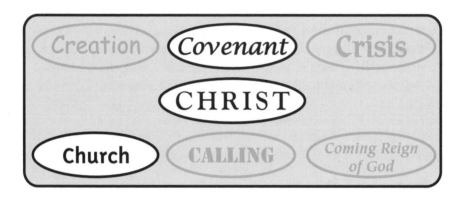

Key Scripture: John 5:39, 46–47

You search the Scriptures because you think that in them you have eternal life; and it is they that testify on my behalf.... If you believed Moses, you would believe me, for he wrote about me. But if you do not believe what he wrote, how will you believe what I say?

We should read the Scriptures with the specific purpose of find-
ing Christ in them. Whoever neglects to do this, even if he wears
himself out through a lifetime of learning, will never reach the
knowledge of the truth. — John Calvin[1]

1. John Calvin, *Commentary on the Gospel of John,* in Alister McGrath and J. I. Packer, eds., Crossway Classic Commentaries Series (Wheaton, Ill.: Crossway Books, 1994), 140.

I want to know one thing, the way to heaven — how to land safe on that happy shore. God himself has condescended to teach the way: for this very end he came from heaven. He hath written it down in a book. O give me that book! At any price give me the Book of God! — John Wesley[2]

Objectives

♦ To learn how to read the Old Testament typologically, meaning that the participants will learn to hear the "echoes of Jesus" in key Old Testament passages.

♦ To understand that the Old Testament and the New Testament are both important for fully grasping the revelation of God in Jesus Christ to the world.

♦ To begin to see how immersing ourselves in the biblical story is a real means of grace that draws us closer to Jesus.

Welcome (2–5 minutes)

As each person arrives, ask about the highlights of the week. As a way to show interest in individuals, ask something like, "Where would you like to make an echo?"

Prayer (3 minutes)

If you have a participant who is comfortable praying aloud, ask him or her to open your time together in prayer.

Whether it is a student or a guide who offers prayer, one option is to use the prayer provided above in "Prepare in Prayer" (page 56).

---

2. John Wesley, "Preface to Sermons on Several Occasions," in *The Bicentennial Edition of the Works of John Wesley,* ed. Albert C. Outler (Nashville: Abingdon Press, 1984), 1:105.

Opener (10–15 minutes)

Begin by saying something like this: Today we're going to focus on ways to read and study the Bible. Take a few moments and consider these three questions:

- Why do we even include the Old Testament in our Bibles?

- Is it important for us to read from the Old Testament, and if so, why?

- What is the relationship between the Old Testament and the New Testament?

Next, give your participants time to think about these questions and write their reflections down on paper. After 5–8 minutes, call everyone together and work through each of the questions, asking participants to tell about what they wrote.

> **Desired result: By searching the Scriptures together participants will begin to hear the echoes of Jesus in the Old Testament stories of Israel.**

Finish up by asking this final question to the whole group, "Can you find Jesus in the Old Testament?" You may get the response that Jesus doesn't show up until the New Testament's four Gospels. Or you may get the response that the coming of Jesus was foretold (for instance, in the passages from Isaiah 7:14 or 9:6–7, mentioned above). Don't be surprised if some of them mention that Jesus, the Word of God — as the second person of the Trinity (Father, Son, and Holy Spirit) — was there at the creation of the heavens and the earth. If someone ventures an answer like that, affirm it wholeheartedly! Guide participants to look at John 1:1–18 about this. (Focus on verses 1–3, 14, and 17–18.) Say something like, "The Word was with God, and the Word was God, in the beginning. Eventually, the Word became flesh, in Jesus. We can discover echoes of this throughout Scripture. Consider the sound of an echo in a canyon, a stadium, or a large room. The sounds seem to bounce around and pop up from a variety of directions. Today we are going to listen for 'echoes of Jesus' in Old Testament stories.'"

Tip: If you have five or fewer participants, you can keep everyone together for the "Echo Explorations."

Echo Explorations (25–45 minutes)

◆ Begin with a short teaching time. Use any material you read in the "Prepare Your Soul," "Prepare Your Mind," and "Prepare Your Heart" sections that you think would be helpful.

Say: "The first Christians looked to the Jewish Scriptures (what later came to be called the Old Testament) to make sense of their faith in Jesus as God's Messiah. Jesus himself began this practice by affirming his mission as the fulfillment of God's plan for his people Israel: 'Do not think that I have come to abolish the law or the prophets,' Jesus preaches in the Sermon on the Mount, 'I have come not to abolish but to fulfill' (Matthew 5:17).

"Because the earliest Christians were Jews, they naturally looked to their own Scriptures to fill out their understanding of Jesus after his resurrection from the dead and ascension into heaven. To put it simply, *they began to hear echoes of Jesus in Old Testament stories that they would not have thought about before.* We see a hint of that in the Gospel of John, where it is written, "His disciples did not understand these things at first; but when Jesus was glorified then they remembered that these things had been written of him and had been done to him" (John 12:16). From a post-resurrection perspective, Jesus' disciples were able to make sense of his life and ministry as the fulfillment of God's promises in a way they could not have done before."

Next, explain: "We are going to explore where to find some of these "echoes of Jesus" in the Old Testament. The word that is often used to describe this way of reading is "prefiguring," meaning that Jesus' life and ministry is prefigured or anticipated in certain Old Testament stories. "Typology" is a way of reading the Bible that focuses on how stories and images in the Old Testament anticipate or prefigure the coming of Jesus as Savior of the world."

Ask one of the participants to read Numbers 21:4–9 aloud to the whole group. Ask:

• How could Jesus be seen in this story?

Then look together at John 3:14–15, which is part of Jesus' conversation with Nicodemus. Point out that Jesus compares the bronze serpent lifted up on the pole by Moses to the way "the Son of Man [must] be lifted up," a reference to his own crucifixion.

• As a next step, divide your group into three smaller groups with an appointed leader for each one. Distribute a handout to each leader; the handouts (Baptism, Bread, Water) can be found on pages 206–208. Decide now whether you form here an advanced group to search the materials in "Advancing Echoes," use it as a take-home, or save it for another meeting. The handout for "Advancing Echoes" can be found on page 209.

Say, "Each group is going to explore an echo of Jesus as it relates to the Old Testament. Read and discuss the Scriptures on the handout."

The leaders should encourage participants to share their thoughts on how the New Testament passage cites the Old Testament passage to illuminate something about Jesus.

• As the final part of the main lesson, call all small groups back together into one big group. Have one volunteer from each group summarize briefly the Old Testament story and New Testament connection that they looked at in their group work.

Say something like, "These connections are just the tip of the iceberg, but that they can help us as Christians get excited about reading the whole Bible."

Advancing Echoes

If you have participants who are ready for a challenge with longer readings, use the Advancing Echoes material about Passover and Crucifixion found in the handout on page 209.

Then the Lord said to Moses, "I am going to rain bread from heaven for you." — Exodus 16:4

Jesus said to them, "I am the bread of life. Whoever comes to me will never be hungry, and whoever believes in me will never be thirsty."
— John 6:35

Activity: Search Your Church (5–10 minutes)

Let participants go through the church to any art or stained-glass windows that are in the sanctuary, chapel, classrooms, etc. Have them look for images from both the Old Testament and the New Testament. Are there any windows where images of the Old and New Testaments are connected in the same window? For example, How might an image of a dove be related to different parts of the Bible?

Reflection

Read the key Scriptures and quotes from Calvin and Wesley on pages 58–59. Ask: "Which one of these best reflects where you are at this point in our session?"

Worship (5–15 minutes)

Say: "When we express God's gift to us of the saving work of Jesus Christ through our worship, we allow the word of God to be 'written on tablets of human hearts' (2 Corinthians 3:3). Through the reading of Scripture, through prayer and praise, and especially through the celebration of the Lord's Supper, we come to a deeper knowledge of God's love for us through Christ Jesus our Lord. And so it is appropriate to close your time in studying the 'echoes of Jesus' throughout the Bible with a time of worship. Hallelujah!"

Conclude your session either with a time of testimony or with singing. Consider using songs that clearly use or refer to Scripture, such as the Third Day song, "Agnus Dei." Mention that the song's title is Latin for "Lamb of God" and that the lyrics are an adaptation of the passage from Revelation 5:6–17, which you may have just read above. Or use another setting of the Agnus Dei (Lamb of God) text. Other hymns and songs you might consider include: "How Firm a Foundation," a traditional hymn available in many hymnals that takes passages of Scripture and presents them as assurances of Jesus to us; "Jerusalem" by Randall Goodgame, "Canaan Bound" by Andrew Peterson, and "Wisdom" by Jill Phillips — contemporary Christian songs that treat biblical images from the Old Testament as proper for Christian worship and devotion.

If you have an ordained pastor available to meet with your youth ministry during this session, you might consider concluding with Eucharist/Holy Communion, especially if you have studied the final set of connections between Passover/Sacrifice and Crucifixion.

Follow-up and Announcements

The wonderful thing about studying the Bible is this: the more you do it, the more familiar you become with the contents of Scripture. And the more you become familiar with Bible stories, the more you want to learn. Meanwhile, you are coming to a deeper knowledge of God through your deeper commitment to God's word.

If you or your youth find that they would like a systematic way to study the Scriptures in their entirety, I have found the following resource particularly helpful:

J. Ellsworth Kalas, *The Grand Sweep: 365 Days from Genesis to Revelation* (Nashville: Abingdon Press, 1996). Dr. Kalas's guide will take you all the way through the Bible in a year. And you only have to read about three chapters a day to do it! He also provides short devotionals to help put each day's reading in context. I have used this guide to read all the way through the Bible on four different occasions, and each time I have learned something new from Dr. Kalas's insightful devotional commentary.

Session 5

The Word: Creative and Poetic
Liz DeGaynor

LEADER PREPARATION

Prepare Your Soul

Have you ever found yourself struck by a powerful turn of phrase, particularly one that you found in Scripture? Such beauty can move the soul to look to God. Even if you are not particularly inspired by poetry, perhaps you have been moved by some aspect of God's creation (e.g., a sunrise, a flower, a waterfall).

What would it take for us to ponder more carefully the poetic words of Scripture?

_____

_____

_____

How could we be more aware of the beauty of God's creation as a poem written anew for us each day?

_____

_____

_____

Spend a few minutes meditating on Psalm 19:1:

> The heavens are telling the glory of God;
> and the firmament proclaims his handiwork.

The Psalmist understood that creation sings praise to God, its Creator. Put this verse into conversation with Lamentations 3:22–24:

The steadfast love of the LORD never ceases,
his mercies never come to an end;
they are new every morning;
great is your faithfulness.
"The LORD is my portion," says my soul,
"therefore I will hope in him."

Consider the possibility that God's abundant love is visibly new to
us every morning with the sunrise and that God offers us frequent
natural reminders throughout the day.

Encourage participants to let go of critical
inclinations and instead just give God an
opening.

Pray something like the following, and then take a walk outside
(or simply look out the window):

*Almighty God, Creator of all things great and small, help me
to be attentive to your handiwork, the tapestry of Nature, in
all of its beauty and complexity. Remind me that I am part of
the weaving by showing me the ways I am connected to You, to
others, and to the world. May I cultivate gratitude in response
to this awareness, through Jesus Christ our Lord, who lives and
reigns with You and the Holy Spirit, now and forever. Amen.*

Allow your eyes to notice what is to be seen.

Enter into a time of prayerful and grateful mediation.

Allow yourself to be silent in order to listen for the voice of God.

Prepare Your Mind

This session invites you and the participants to be thoughtful and attentive to words and images. There are resources listed at the end of this
unit that you may want to use in preparation for the activities. Listen to
some of the suggested music. Spend some time looking over the Scripture passages and the poems. Begin to respond to some of the questions

or discussion prompts for yourself and begin to formulate questions and discussion prompts that might be useful for your particular group.

Prepare Your Heart

As your group enters into reflection about creation and enters into creative responses to words of Scripture, be open to the movement of the Holy Spirit in all of those who are present. Some people may have difficulty with Scripture, with poetry, or with the process of artistic creation. Others may be energized and inspired. Try to create a space of safety and hospitality that allows room for divine action and personal work; also cultivate acceptance for those who might resist the activities.

> Why not invite other leaders to join you in the preparation of Soul, Mind, and Heart?

Prepare Your Space

This session could be done outside (under a shady tree in a park, perhaps). Think about places of natural beauty where your participants could walk around individually and could also sit together. Wouldn't that be great? If there are obstacles to getting outdoors, try to create an indoor space that is filled with visual images of nature (photographs, works of art, plants, etc.). You may also want to use music to set the mood (see Resources on page 73).

Prepare Your Supplies

* Bibles.

* Copies of the handouts.

* Paper and writing utensils.

* A guitar or a piano for the music (or a music player and CDs).

Prepare Your Publicity

People are often drawn to Beauty. Use striking images of creation to garner interest. Make posters or fliers using Scripture references (such as those above) that connect to those images.

Prepare Your Plan

Bring the adults who will be joining you for this session up to speed. Perhaps you could do the Soul/Heart/Mind Preparation together.

Prepare Further

For background information about the connections between poetry and Scripture, see Robert Alter's *The Art of Biblical Poetry* (Basic Books, 1985) and *Sweet Jesus: Poems about the Ultimate Icon,* ed. Nic Carbo and Denise Duhamel (Anthology Press, 2002). For good examples of poets who engage God's word, see Denise Levertov and John Donne.

TEMPLATE FOR SESSION FIVE
The Word: Creative and Poetic

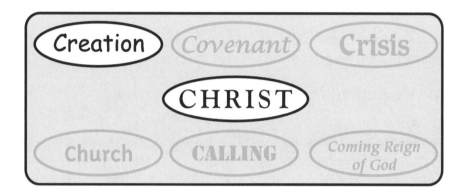

Key Biblical Phrase:

The heavens are telling the glory of God; and the firmament proclaims His handiwork. (Psalm 19:1)

Key Scriptures: Psalms 8, 19, 104, and 148

Objectives

- To experience the power of poetry in Scripture.

- To deepen our appreciation of poetic language, including that which is found in Scripture.

- To encourage us to see nature as God's poetry.

All creation is a song of praise to God.
— Hildegard of Bingen, twelfth-century mystic

Preparation (10–15 minutes)

Before participants enter, have the space prepared. If you are outside, you may want to lay out blankets. If you are inside, try to bring the outside in with images from nature. You may also want to set the mood by having tranquil music playing.

Gathering (5–10 minutes)

As participants arrive, invite them to go for a quick walk around the space, being quietly attentive to what they see, hear, and feel.

Welcome and Opening Prayer (3–5 minutes)

After you have gathered everyone together, welcome them and say something like, "Creation is God's artistic masterpiece. Some appreciate it visually, while others are attuned to the music of the spheres. Some take a hold of it tactilely, and others write words of praise and thanksgiving. Today, I hope we will have the opportunity to experience nature as God's poetry and to deepen our appreciation for poetic words that have been written in gratitude to God. Then you will be invited to respond by creating your own poetry."

> *Leader:* The Lord be with you.
>
> *Group:* And also with you.

> *Leader: Let us pray ... [feel free to say the following or to offer your own variation]. God of all creation, who called into being all that is in the heavens above and on the earth below, we thank you for this beautiful gift. Give us eyes to see your handiwork, ears to hear creation's song of praise to you, minds and hearts that are open to appreciating your artistry, and hands to create our own responses of gratitude. Through Jesus Christ, who lives and reigns with you in the unity of the Holy Spirit. Amen.*

Poems in the Bible (10–20 minutes)

Say something like: "We've already spent some time looking at God's creation. Now let's turn to biblical and poetic words written in response to it. The word 'poem' comes from the Greek word *poema*, which means 'creation.' Since 'poem' and 'creation' are connected, it may not surprise us that people over time and across cultures have viewed creation as a poem. We've talked before about the three persons of the Trinity, but we may not have discussed that Jesus Christ is also known as 'Logos' (meaning 'word' in Greek), which is translated into English as 'Word' in many Bibles. Listen to John 1:1–3b .'In the beginning was the Word, and the Word was with God, and the Word was God. He was in the beginning with God. All things came into being through him, and without him not one thing came into being.' Notice how the author of John explains that Jesus was not only present at creation, but was a crucial component of the creative process. Some theologians (folks who study God) argue that Jesus, as the Divine Word, spoke creation into being. We see the language of spoken creation in Genesis 1: 'And God said. . . . ' This would seem to imply that words matter, right?

> John Calvin describes the Psalms as "an anatomy of all the parts of the soul," believing that they "will principally teach and train us to bear the cross."

"One way of defining theology is as conversation about God. As we turn to poetry that praises the God of creation, let us be attentive to the words.

"Let's begin with a few examples from the book of Psalms, the longest collection of poems we have in the Bible. It contains words of lament and sorrow, words of anger and doubt, words of thanksgiving and praise. Today we are going to consider Psalms that focus on God's creation. As we explore these poems, pay attention to the words and how they are used to paint images along with offering praise."

Note: There are four Psalms offered: Psalms 8, 19, 104, and 148. You may want to focus on one with everyone together. After a collective discussion, you may want to divide students into smaller groups to explore the others. Handouts can be found on pages 211–215.

Poetry Touching the Divine (10–20 minutes)

Say: "Now let's move on to other poems."

Note: There are three poems offered. You may choose to focus on only one of them or to use all of them individually or collectively. The handouts of the poems can be found on pages 216–219.

Reflection/Worship (15–30 minutes)

One of the ways for us to reflect on the splendor of creation and the words of poetry written to praise God the Creator is for us to respond with our creative gifts. Perhaps you will want to write a poem. You could also draw a picture. Perhaps you will want to compose some music. Perhaps you will want to choreograph a dance. These are all acts of worship and praise. Spend some time enacting your God-given gifts as an offering back to God.

Let participants offer their work in praise of God the Creator. Spend some time singing a few creation-related songs together as an act of worship (see the Resources section on the following page.

> Poetry is an intensive use of words as maximal speech. — George Steiner

Closing Prayer

You may want to close by reading one of the Psalms responsively. Or you could pray something like this:

God of creation, you have woven a tapestry of beauty in nature, with many colors and textures. You sustain even the places where we have soiled or ripped the fabric. We live in hope of creation's complete restoration when Christ returns. You love each element of creation, including us. Just as the heavens and the hills sing with joy, we offer songs of praise. Just as the fields produce food for harvest, we offer artistic gifts in reponse to thank you for your abundant grace. Help us to be mindful of your creation that we may attend to it without neglect or abuse.

Help us also to be aware of one another as being created in your image. May your steadfast love empower us to love one another, in the name of the Triune God, Father, Son, and Holy Spirit. Amen.

Follow-up

- Notice which participants display specific artistic gifts. Find out about the artists in your congregation or area and pair them up (e.g., for future workshops).
- Check for artistic offerings in your town. Take the group to a museum or a concert. Chat about art, beauty, and God afterward.
- Schedule a time for the group to go out walking in nature.

Resources

Robert Alter, *The Art of Biblical Poetry* (Basic Books, 1985).

Nic Carbo and Denise Duhamel, eds., *Sweet Jesus: Poems about the Ultimate Icon* (Anthology Press, 2002).

Emilie Griffin, ed., *A Syllable of Water: Twenty Writers of Faith Reflect on the Art* (Paraclete Press, 2008).

Related to Psalms

Eugene Peterson, *Answering God: The Psalms as Tools for Prayer* (Harper & Row, 1989). An accessible "user's manual" to the Psalter, from a scholar with decades of pastoral experience.

J. David Pleins, *The Psalms: Songs of Tragedy, Hope, and Justice* (Orbis Books, 1993). A study using lenses of social justice and liberation theology.

Laurance Wieder, *Words to God's Music* (Eerdmans, 2003). Renders the Psalms into English poetry.

Related to Music

For Psalms set to folk music, see Charles Pettee's CD *Steadfast Love.*

Classical Suggestions

Haydn, "The Creation"

Vivaldi, "The Four Seasons"

From the United Methodist Hymnal *and the* New Century Hymnal

"All Creatures of Our God and King" (*UMH* #62), *NCH* #17
"For the Beauty of the Earth" (*UMH* #92), *NCH* #28)
"Morning Has Broken" (*UMH* #145)
"This Is My Father's World" (*UMH* #144)
*www.gbod.org/worship/default.asp?loc_id=17,482,485&act
=nav_loc.* Music resources connected with the United Methodist Church.

Other Hymns

*www.blaynechastain.com/files/webfm/downloads/pdf/we-sing-the
.pdf.* This website has the lyrics and music for "We Sing the Greatness of Our God" by Isaac Watts.
www.hymnary.org/tune/earth_and_all_stars. This website has the lyrics and music for "Earth and All Stars" by David N. Johnson.

Contemporary Praise

*http://i-worship.blogspot.com/2008/08/creation-calls-brian-doerksen
.html.* This website has lyrics, music, and a video for "Creation Calls" by Brian Doerksen.
www.musicnotes.com/sheetmusic/mtd.asp?ppn=MN0050990.
This website has the lyrics and guitar chords for "God of Wonders" by Third Day and Caedmon's Call.
www.youtube.com/watch?v=1CBNE25rtnE. This website contains a video of "God of Wonders" by Third Day and Caedmon's Call — lots of natural imagery.

Part Two

BATH

Session 6

Baptismal Imaginings: Water as Symbol, Story, and Theology for the Church

Fred P. Edie

LEADER PREPARATION

Prepare Your Soul

Pray this devotional prayer, or one of your own.

> *Dear God, you give us life, sustenance, signs, and symbols. As I prepare to lead this exploration of the beauty of baptism, give me an awareness of how you fill us with the Holy Spirit. Use me, I pray, as you used John to invite people to "prepare the way of the Lord." (Mark 1:3)*

Read Matthew 3:16–17

What does this scriptural passage say to you?

_____

_____

_____

What do you wonder about it?

_____

_____

_____

What do you know or recall (or anticipate) of your own baptism?

_____

_____

_____

Imagine who might have been present and their facial expressions.

_____

_____

_____

What's your favorite use of water in daily life?

_____

_____

_____

How could that connect you with or remind you of God's love and grace?

_____

_____

_____

Those who are baptized in Christ are a new creation! (2 Corinthians 5:17)

Prepare Your Mind

Baptisms come and go in our churches, sometimes barely rippling the surface of our collective consciousness. This session is about re-imagining and re-membering the significance of the Christian baptism we practice. Instead of rehashing tired arguments about how wet we should get and when we should get wet, however, students will be invited to think deeply about the power of water as religious symbol; about the organic connections between baptismal practices and the stories of God's salvation found in the Bible; and about the breadth of theological meaning enacted through baptism.

Did You Say "Just"?

Symbols, like the liturgy that puts them into play, are often preceded by the word "just." "It's just a symbol," or "That's just a ritual," we exclaim cynically, as if the realm of holy mystery exists somewhere beyond these earthly things and our ordinary practices of them. Incarnation means, however, that God's *extraordinary* saving presence may be communicated through *ordinary* water in a commonplace bath. One dimension of this grace offered through baptism is the incorporation of the baptized into the sweep of God's saving history, which stretches from the beginning of time to the life, death, and resurrection of Jesus Christ and points toward the fulfillment of God's promised future.

In other words, *to be baptized is to be blessed with a story and an identity as one who is part of God's plan of salvation!* Further, to be baptized also means being grafted into a theological tradition, a way of making sense of life on earth in relation to God. It turns out that the church's earliest theologians, the writers of the Book, were already hard at work reflecting on the theological meanings of baptism. Thus, in this session the group will be invited to explore connections between the baptismal bath and such theological themes as Creation, Covenant, Crisis, Christ, Church, Calling, and the Coming Reign of God (that is, our Alliterative C's; see the diagram on page 84).

Prepare Your Heart

Students are formed in school to care most about rational and empirical ways of understanding the world. Lost from our awareness is the power and influence of the human heart. Unlike Mr. Spock, a *Star Trek* character whose decisions were influenced solely by logic, it is our hearts (and not merely reason or science) that often motivate us to act; it is our hearts that lead us to open up to God's love or reach out to our neighbors with compassion. This session (indeed, this entire book) focuses on cultivating capacities of the heart as an essential means to listening for God's communication and responding to the promptings of God's Holy Spirit.

Symbols hold the capacity to stir our hearts if we learn how to attend to them. Water is a case in point. In my own life, I've delighted in the refreshment of cold water after hard work on a hot summer's day, exulted in learning to race across ocean waters on a sailboard, fled from the tidal surge of a hurricane, and, once, nearly drowned. These memories are freighted with emotion. Thus, when I'm brought into proximity with the waters of the baptismal font at worship, all these memories and the multivalent emotions associated with them come with me. Whether I'm conscious of them or not, God can make God's presence known through these feelings deeper than words.

What are your own memorable encounters with water?

_____

_____

_____

What can these encounters teach you about the gift and power of your baptism?

_____

_____

_____

Where has the grace of your baptism overflowed into love and compassion for God and the world?

_____

_____

_____

Where have you seen such overflowing through your students?

_____

_____

_____

Prepare Your Space

- Arrange the teaching space by setting chairs in a semicircular pattern facing a writing board or newsprint on an easel. Plan to break the large semicircle into smaller clusters of chairs for small group Bible study.

- If you have access to one, an (understated) indoor fountain can contribute to the learning environment. You will need to set it up ahead of time somewhere prominent in the space.

- If you plan to use either A or B in the Invitations to Engagement, you will need to acquire and set up the requisite technology or arrange for access to the water feature ahead of time.

Prepare Your Supplies

- Board or newsprint with markers.

- Laptop computer, projector, screen, and necessary cables (if choosing Invitation to Engagement A).

- Unimpeded access to natural or constructed water feature (if choosing Invitation to Engagement B).

- Bibles (one for each student), paper and pencils for notes.

Prepare Your Plan

The primary components of this session are included in the three main movements:

- Imagining water as a religious symbol.

- Connecting the bath, the book, and us to the Stories of God's Salvation.

- Swimming in baptismal waters, immersed in theology.

These are the movements you should focus on if you have 60 minutes or less. Otherwise, the session will last between 90 minutes and 2 hours. Of course, you may easily extend this material over two meetings. In this longer time frame you will have the opportunity to do more of the work that assists in forming students' spiritual and theological imaginations (Invitation to Engagement, Options A or B, for example, or Worship, Option B).

This material is wonderfully rich in content; therefore, your own prior consideration of the movements, especially the Scriptures and the theology within them, is vital. Students will be encouraged when they sense that you are already invested in their learning. Consider scheduling this and other sessions on baptism in close connection with actual occasions of baptism in your congregation or on baptismal festival days (e.g., Baptism of the Lord, Easter, Pentecost).

Prepare Your Publicity

• Use images of water to elicit interest in this event. A garden hose, rainstorm, water well, or baptismal font could work.

• Offer teaser questions in your publicity, such as "What does getting wet have to do with getting God?"

• Set up a kiddie pool in the church parking lot with a sign announcing the topic, time, and place. Have the group prepare simple invitations or flyers and distribute them nearby.

Prepare in Prayer

Gracious God, you provide us water to...

_____

_____

_____

Using the mind you've given, I prayerfully ponder the myriad meanings of my baptism...

_____

_____

_____

I pray for these people in our group...

_____

_____

_____

Lead me as I seek to lead them. Empower me as I seek to empower them for ministry. Remind us how we are washed in your grace and love in Jesus Christ. Amen.

Prepare Further

Baptism, Eucharist and Ministry (World Council of Churches, 1982; available online).

Fred Edie, *Book, Bath, Table, and Time: Christian Worship as Source and Resource for Youth Ministry* (Pilgrim Press, 2007). See especially pages 132–43 in chapter 5, "Contemplating the Bath."

Laurence Hull Stookey, *Baptism: Christ's Act in the Church* (Abingdon, 1982).

TEMPLATE FOR SESSION SIX
Baptismal Imaginings: Water as Symbol, Story, and Theology for the Church

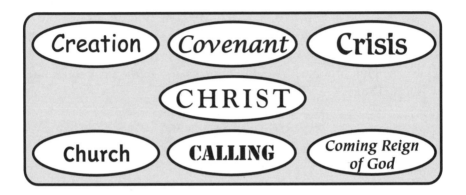

Key Scripture: Matthew 3:16–17

And when Jesus had been baptized, just as he came up from the water, suddenly the heavens were opened to him and he saw the Spirit of God descending like a dove and alighting on him. And a voice from heaven said, "This is my Son, the Beloved, with whom I am well pleased."

Objectives

- To learn to live richly out of our baptismal faith.

- To imagine the multiple meanings of water as a religious symbol.

- To learn how the church connected baptism with its stories of salvation.

- To consider the theological meanings of baptism.

- To cultivate the capacity of the heart for engaging ritual symbols.

Welcome (5–10 minutes)

Say: "Welcome! Let's dive in! Please form pairs or trios and share stories of significant encounters with water." If examples would be helpful to prime the pump, offer ideas such as washing, rain, ocean, global needs for clean drinking water, water to quench drought, playing in a sprinkler, etc. After a few minutes, ask one or two volunteers (or more if time allows) to share their encounters.

Say: "In this session, we attempt to 'dive in' to the power and meaning of Christian baptism. Hopefully, you will emerge a stronger swimmer in Christ's baptismal waters."

Opener / Invitation to Engagement, Option A: View a Media Presentation Featuring Water

(10–15 minutes)

Supplies: laptop computer with Internet access and multimedia presentation software, projector, cables, screen.

Create, or invite a student to create, ahead of time a short (2–4 minute) montage of water-related images and/or sounds. Royalty free downloads are readily available on the Internet. Search on "water images" or "water sounds." These may be arranged in a Power Point or slide presentation or, for the technologically savvy, edited into a moving video presentation.

Alternative: Show a DVD recording of moving water, such as the beach or a river. Show it with a computer or DVD player and television screen. This activity could also be done using a large photograph of water, such as a calendar photo or a photo in a coffee table book.

Say: "As you watch this brief presentation, meditate on the images, memories, feelings, and meanings of water that are evoked inside you."

After viewing the presentation, ask questions like these:

+ How did you feel as this presentation began? How did you feel during it, and at the end?

+ What memories are evoked for you?

+ What aspects of our life with water seem important to you now?

Opener / Invitation to Engagement, Option B: Reflect on Living Water (10–15 minutes)

Supplies/preparation: relatively undisturbed access to a water feature.

Invite students to gather around a natural or human-made (running) water feature. Say: "In silence and on your own utilize all your senses to 'take in' or meditate on this water. Pay attention to the images, memories, feelings, and meanings evoked inside you."

Note: More time can be allowed if the water is particularly interesting and worthy of lengthy consideration — exploring a waterfall, for example.

After engaging in this meditative exercise, ask questions like these:

+ What senses are engaged by your encounter with water?
+ What images or memories came to mind as you meditated?
+ What feelings did the water stir in you?

Main Movements / Exercise One: Imagine Water as a Religious Symbol (12–15 minutes)

Supplies: Marker board or newsprint, marker

Say: "In this exercise, you are invited to explore the deep significance of water for life on earth as well as the symbolic power of the waters of baptism for your life in Christian community. We begin by brainstorming the human significance of water."

Write the heading "Human Significance of H_2O" at the top of a marker board or newsprint. Say: "Let's list some examples of the significance of water." Invite students to call out responses. A leader or assistant should record them. Examples include (but are not limited to) birth, life, death, power, cleansing, solvent, recreation, transport, work, disaster, peace, terror, awe, transformation, judgment, and healing.

Say: "Now, as you ponder our list, listen as I read this definition of a 'religious symbol.' Religious symbols are objects of human experience that (1) gather around themselves multiple and even contradictory meanings; (2) affect us emotionally (in our hearts) as well as in our minds; and (3) carry moral significance, that is, they cast a vision of right and wrong." Ask:

- Looking back over the list, where do you see evidence of multiple and even contradictory meanings for water?
- What emotions have we named that water may stir in us?
- How might the meanings of water be related to issues of right and wrong?

Say: "As far back as New Testament times, the church recognized that water was already a powerful religious symbol. The church's inspiration was to take these symbolic meanings of water in general and to interpret them in light of the waters of Christian baptism." Ask:

- What connections do you see between this list we've created and baptismal themes from Christian faith?

  Note: This question may be difficult for some. Consider how you may assist students in making connections like these.

- Just as the deep water of the ocean can mean death for a person, the waters of baptism mean death to the old sinful self. This is a form of judgment.
- Just as we use water to cleanse our hands or wash a wound, the waters of baptism mean cleansing from sin. This is a form of healing.
- The waters of baptism involve re-creation, new birth, and new life in Jesus Christ.
- The waters of baptism dissolve old boundaries that formerly separated persons from one another and transport us into a new community (the church) and toward God's promised, Coming Reign.
- The waters of baptism "mix us together" with God and other Christians in a covenant that lasts for our entire lives.
- As a rainstorm evokes our feelings, the baptismal waters are capable of stirring our hearts to terror, awe, joy, and peace.

After you've prompted student reflections along these lines summarize with this statement: "Nearly everything we can say about water as a religious symbol generally, the church claimed by analogy for its waters of baptism in a specific Christian theological sense."

Main Movements / Exercise Two A:
Connecting the Bath, the Book, and Us
to the Stories of God's Salvation (12–15 minutes)

Supplies: Marker board or newsprint, appropriate marker, Bibles.

Say: "In this exercise we explore the significance of water in the Bible. As with the first move, we'll brainstorm together. First, let's remember some of the Old Testament stories related to water. In a moment we'll turn to the New Testament."

Record or have an assistant write student responses for all to see.

Note: If your students are unfamiliar with the Bible you may wish to have them work in pairs or trios with Bibles before writing responses on the board.

Old Testament Partial List

• Creation

• Noah

• Moses (basket in bull rushes, plagues, deliverance through the Red Sea, striking rock)

• crossing Jordan into Promised Land

• Elijah stories

• Jonah

New Testament Partial List

• Jesus born through water of mother's womb, healed with water, taught from water, calmed seas, walked on water, turned water into wine, described as living water, water flows from his side

• baptisms in Acts

* Paul's missionary journeys across Mediterranean

* imagery of God's coming Reign in Revelation 22:1–5 features waters of the River of Life flowing toward the Heavenly City.

Say: "Notice how water 'flows like a fugal theme' (Aidan Kavanagh) through the entire biblical story from the very beginning of time through the life, death, and resurrection of Jesus Christ and even through the imagery for God's coming Reign. The ancient church noticed this too and quickly came to associate baptism with all these stories. Thus, to be baptized was to be given a new story, the story of God's salvation.

> Nearly everything we can say about water as a religious symbol generally, the church claimed by analogy for its waters of baptism in a specific Christian theological sense.

"To be baptized was to be made part of a community that possessed a storied history with God. To be baptized was to be made a descendant of Noah, Moses, Miriam, Mary, Jesus, Paul, and Phoebe. Moreover, in many traditions, the occasion of baptism was understood to be the *re-presenting* and *re-membering* of those stories to the worshiping community. It was as if all God's past saving action was being accomplished all over again in the moment of baptism. One church father could describe it only as 'awesome.' "

Main Movements / Exercise Two B:
Explore an Ancient Baptismal Prayer (15 minutes)

Supplies: Handouts of the ancient baptismal prayer (page 220).

> *Note:* You may use this prayer here and/or in the closing worship portion of the session.

Distribute copies of the handout (page 220). Read aloud the discussion questions to assist participants in their listening or invite a student to read aloud the excerpt from the ancient baptismal prayer. Explain that this is a prayer that the Orthodox Church continues to use today in its baptismal services and at festivals celebrating Jesus' baptism by John.

In response to the reading ask discussion questions like these:

* What imagery does the prayer use?
* What biblical stories does it remember?
* What theological convictions does it voice?
* What emotions does it seek to evoke?
* Why does it use "today" in reference to events that occurred six hundred years earlier?

  (Hint: This is consistent with the claim that the use of "today" expresses the conviction that in baptism God's salvation is re-presented (presented again and anew) not merely represented, and it is re-membered, not merely remembered. This pushes us to regard baptism as an occasion for God to *act* powerfully, if mystically, in the present day.)

What does Jesus' use of the word "today" in Luke 4:21 and 23:43 mean to you now?

Main Movements / Exercise Three: Swimming in Baptismal Waters, Paddling in Theology (25–30 minutes)

Supplies: Marker board or newsprint and markers, Bibles.

Say: "In Exercise One we explored how the church made use of the powerful symbol of water in its sacrament of baptism. In Exercise Two we explored how the church came to understand the sacrament of baptism as incorporation into the saving stories of God collected in the book (Bible). In Exercise Three, we consider what the practice of baptism means theologically."

♦ Go over the **"Alliterative C's"**

Write the following terms for all to see:

> Creation
> Covenant
> Crisis
> Christ
> Church
> Calling
> Coming Reign of God

Say: "These are theological terms. Theology is the word for the church's and our own thinking about what it means to live our lives together with God. Thus *Creation* speaks to God's loving power and our own grateful receipt of the gift of life. *Covenant* describes how God binds God's self to us and ourselves to God in love. *Crisis* names our sinful disobedience and ingratitude. *Christ* brings new *Creation*, new *Covenant*, new life to us. The *Church* is Christ's body in the world at present. Our *Calling* is to share in Christ's ministry. And we look for Christ's return heralding God's *Coming Reign*. In a nutshell, these *Alliterative C's* name nearly every major theological theme of the Christian faith."

Say: "In this exercise, we explore how the church's practice of baptism participates in and enacts dimensions of these theological themes. We will read biblical texts related to baptism and then note how their writers may be reflecting theologically on the meaning of the practices of baptism by linking them to one or more of the Alliterative C's. We'll do the first one together."

♦ Read or invite a student to read aloud Matthew 3:13–4:1. You may choose to use Readers' Theater for this passage. If so, you will need voices for the narrator, John, Jesus, and God. See page 15 for another example of Readers' Theater.

After reading the passage say: "Remember, we're approaching the passage theologically. We're treating it like far more than a newspaper report. We're assuming that Matthew, besides telling the story of Jesus' baptism by John, is also signaling theologically what he thinks baptism *means*. To help us decode his thinking, keep in mind the Alliterative C's."

Ask questions like the following to stimulate participants' theological reflection. Since this practice may be unfamiliar to many participants, you may need to lead them a bit at this point.

• Besides Jesus and John, what are the three essential ingredients to Jesus' baptism? (water, Spirit of God, voice of God)

• Where do these three ingredients show up together in the Old Testament? (very beginning of Genesis 1 account of creation)

• What is Matthew signaling theologically? (refer to the Alliterative C's on the board) (Baptism is linked to creation. Christ as inaugurating new creation)

• Where in the Old Testament does the dove appear? (Noah story, Genesis 8)

• By linking baptism to Noah what is Matthew signaling? (Dove returns to Noah with "evidence of creation renewed," implying new creation for and new covenant with Noah and his descendants. Baptism linked again to creation and also to covenant.)

• After his baptism and through his struggle with Satan (chapter 4 of Matthew) what is Jesus working out? (His baptismal calling, the nature of his identity as God's son (messiah Christ) and the shape of his ministry)

Summarize: While pointing to the list of Alliterative C's, say, "In this brief passage Matthew not only tells the story of Jesus' baptism by John but signals that to be baptized has theological implications for us including creation, covenant, and calling." Ask:

• "What piece of Matthew's theology of baptism is new or intriguing to you?"

Next, divide students into pairs or small groups to explore the biblical passages that follow. Assign one or two passages to each group: Romans 6:3–11; Galatians 3:26–28; 2 Corinthians 5:17–20; Revelation 22:1–5; Colossians 2:20–3:15; 1 Corinthians 12:12–27.

Write for all to see: (1) links to baptism.
(2) which Alliterative C's?

Instruct them: (1) to look for evidence that links these passages to the practice of baptism and (2) to reflect on what theological meaning of baptism is being explored in light of the Alliterative C's. After 10 minutes or so, invite students to report their findings. As the groups summarize their findings, highlight the following:

Romans 6:3–11
Baptism into life, death, and resurrection of Jesus **Christ,** freedom from **crisis** of sin.

Galatians 3:26–28
Church's unity in Christ dissolves distinctions rooted in class, race, gender.

2 Corinthians 5:17–20
Those "in Christ" (baptized) are new **creations.** The baptized are called to share in Christ's **calling** (ministry) of reconciliation.

Revelation 22:1–5
Coming Reign of God depicted with imagery of life-giving water.

Colossians 2:20–3:15
Character of people who share in baptismal **covenant.**

1 Corinthians 12:12–27
Giftedness, callings of individual members of Christ's body, the **church.**

Recap: "Together we've explored how the writers of the Scriptures were working out the theological significance of baptism as it was being practiced in their churches. In light of the symbolic power of water, the linkage of water to God's saving activity, and now the wide and deep theological implications for baptism, you can see better what is at stake in your own baptism. Clearly, to be baptized was more than a silly ritual at an isolated moment in a person's life; it was a Way of Life in communion with Christ's body."

Worship / Option A:
Pray Together the Prayer Excerpt
from Sophronios of Jerusalem (2–10 minutes)

Supplies: copies of the baptismal prayer. Handout 1 for Session 6 on page 220.

Distribute copies and set a worshipful mood, perhaps by dimming the lights or moving to a chapel, sanctuary, or other worship location. You could also gather near the baptismal font or pour water into a bowl in your meeting space.

Pray the prayer in unison, or ask various participants to lead a section each.

Worship / Option B:
Participate in a Service of Baptismal Renewal
(20–60 minutes)

At present many denominational hymnals and books of worship contain services of baptismal renewal. You could invite an ordained clergyperson to plan such a service with your group. Students may be engaged as readers of Scripture, prayers of prayers, singers of songs or to testify to their deepened engagement with water and the sacrament. The minister may wish to preach and will lead the baptismal renewal liturgy. Make sure the service affords everyone the opportunity to see and touch the baptismal waters as a means to recommit themselves to deepened life in Christ.

Follow-up

+ Invite students to attend to how they interpret their subsequent encounters with water baptismally.

+ Invite students to make the sign of the cross each day in the shower and to say in the tradition of Martin Luther: "Thank God I am baptized."

+ Reflect with students after a baptism in worship on how they encountered it differently as a result of your baptismal imaginings together.

+ Inform your pastors about how this session went and what it brought up for participants. Inform your pastor if there is anyone who might desire more conversation about baptism or who might seek to prepare for Christian baptism.

Session 7

Dreaming for Change: Part I
Sarah Arthur

This is a two-part session that could be done as two 60–90 minute segments for a weekly youth group or small group, or over the course of a retreat weekend. It also could be done as a three-hour visioning retreat, perhaps on a Saturday morning.

Key Scripture: Colossians 1:9–10

For this reason, since the day we heard it, we have not ceased praying for you and asking that you may be filled with the knowledge of God's will in all spiritual wisdom and understanding, so that you may lead lives worthy of the Lord, fully pleasing to him, as you bear fruit in every good work and as you grow in the knowledge of God.

> ...that you may be filled with the knowledge of God's will. — Colossians 1:9

LEADER PREPARATION

Prepare Your Soul

- If you were to write a letter to this group of youth, what would you tell them?

_____

_____

_____

◆ What do you want them to know about God and their Christian calling?

_____

_____

_____

◆ What prayers, hopes, dreams, and fears do you have for them?

_____

_____

_____

Read Philippians 1:9 – 11

The Apostle Paul knew just what it feels like to be both burdened and excited for a growing group of believers. The letters to the Ephesians, Philippians, and Colossians begin with prayers that sound very similar. He prays that they may be given "a spirit of wisdom and revelation as you come to know [God]" (Ephesians 1:17), that they be given "knowledge and full insight" in order "to determine what is best" (Philippians 1:9–10), so that they "may lead lives worthy of the Lord, fully pleasing to [God]" (Colossians 1:10).

In fact, the whole goal of this spiritual journey is to grow in love for God so that we will have the ability to discern the unique ministry that God has in store for us. The goal is Christian discernment — and not just as individuals, but together, as the body of Christ. In particular, *God is calling your church, through your youth,* to respond to a particular problem or concern in your community, such as job losses, foreclosures, homelessness, toxic waste, AIDS, child abuse, violence in schools. Isn't it exciting that you get to be "in" on what God is doing to address those issues?

Prepare Your Mind

Youth can be just the sort of visionary, discerning people that the Apostle Paul prays about in his letters. Often they have a strong sense of injustice (how many times have you heard, "But it's not fair!"?), and yet they still are able to dream without censoring themselves

(adults are much more prone to say, "But this is the way we've always done it" or "But we don't have the money for that.")

The "Alliterative C's" (see Session 6) offer participants an awareness of several key things: First, we don't go it alone. We are part of the *Church,* the body of believers that stretches through time and space. This church throughout history has had a habit of dreaming for change and making change happen. Second, through *baptism,* God is *Calling* (Alliterative C) each of us to a unique vocation and ministry. We will not rest until we respond to that call. Third, through the promise of Scripture, the creeds, and the sacrament of communion, we are assured of the *Coming Reign of God* (Alliterative C). The world will not always be a mess. As a body of believers, we are called to step into that Coming Reign by doing the work of God's realm in the here and now.

We step into God's work by practicing discernment. The Apostle Paul's prayers for the churches indicate that discernment is a vital task of the church if it is to grow in faithfulness and fruitfulness. We don't just get together to have fun and be "family": we are called to listen to what God wants us to do together. The church as the body of Christ has tremendous power — the same power that raised Christ from the dead (Ephesians 1:20). There's a sense in which we are greater than the sum of our parts. Our response together as a congregation to a problem facing our community can be much more powerful than any one of us trying to respond alone.

The question is, How do we know what God is calling us to? Must we respond to every problem that comes our way? Or is there some problem in particular that God wants us to address, using our unique gifts as a congregation?

In Sessions 7 and 8 participants will practice discernment about one issue in particular (and how to respond to it) through the exercises of contemplative prayer, Bible study, discussion, and consensus-building.

Prepare Your Heart

As the group engages in discernment about an area of concern in your community, be mindful of participants or leaders whose problems have been made public lately (e.g., divorce notices in the newspaper, arrests, etc.). Also be aware that as concerns are discussed, there may be certain issues not raised or addressed because the church or this particular gathering may not feel like a safe place in which to be open. Be aware of the nonverbal communication of participants in the group who may seem to be uncomfortable, tuning out, angry, or unusually quiet. Please show the love of Christ in how you attend to them. Consider ways to follow up with them in private afterward.

Prepare Your Space

For these two sessions, a youth room with couches or comfortable chairs is ideal, as is plenty of wall space for poster work. If possible, situate seating roughly in a circle. If you choose to do the prayer walk exercise (page 105), you may want to utilize space that is near the heart of your community or city. Or if you choose to do the prayer tour exercise (page 105), you will need to reserve a van or line up drivers for roughly one hour, depending on how large your community is and how much time you have.

Prepare Your Supplies

For Part 1 (Session 7):

- A week's worth of local newspapers (or ask someone to collect them for you).
- Tape.
- Scissors (a pair for every two or three participants).
- Poster paper or newsprint (enough for six to eight large posters).
- Plain scrap paper or printer paper (several sheets for each participant).
- Three to five colored pencils for each participant.
- Pens or pencils (one for each participant).
- Washable markers or crayons (at least one for each participant).
- Bibles (at least one for each pair, preferably one for each participant).
- *Optional:* candles and matches or lighter; music player with gentle instrumental music and speakers.

For Part 2 (Session 8):

+ Bibles.

+ Pens or pencils.

+ Washable markers.

+ Poster paper or newsprint.

+ Candle and matches or lighter.

+ Hymnals or song sheets for the closing liturgy.

Prepare Your Plan

Make sure your adult leaders or other helpers are aware of the format for these two sessions, especially if your group is not familiar with contemplative prayer practices. Through the practice of silence and contemplation, you are stepping into an ancient Christian practice in which the Holy Spirit has been known to show up. What you are offering the youth is a gift they are not often given at school or home. Who knows what will happen in the process?

Keep your pastor and other church leaders aware of the possible outcome of these sessions, which (hopefully!) will be a concrete action plan for responding to a concern or problem in your local community. Tell them that participants will be coming to them to present the ideas they have discerned in prayer and consensus-building. Ask them to pray for the process in advance. In particular, it is quite possible that the participants will identify a problem that directly involves the missions or outreach teams of your church, so those leaders may also need to be made aware.

Do your best to let the discernment and decisions be led by God at the intersection of the leading of the Holy Spirit and the interests and life experiences of the participants. That is, be careful not to convey that a direction or decision has already been determined.

Prepare Your Publicity

In your printed and verbal communications inviting people to this event, use phrases like these:

+ God's Plan Is on the Way!

+ Urgent: Community Needs Our Church!

◆ We're Gonna Make a Real Difference. Don't Miss It.

◆ Ever Want to Change the World? We Start Next Sunday.

Prepare in Prayer

Take a moment and pray one of Paul's prayers on behalf of your youth and your church: Ephesians 1:16–20; Philippians 1:9–11; or Colossians 1:9–11. Pause with each phrase and think of how it applies specifically to your context. Then pray for the wisdom to guide this process of discernment for and with your youth. Jot down your own prayers here:

_____

_____

_____

Prepare Further

For background and ideas on Christian practices of discernment with youth, see chapter 8, "Plunging In: Baptismal Vocation and Youth's Ministry" in Fred Edie's *Book, Book, Table, and Time.*

See also:

David F. White, *Practicing Discernment with Youth* (Pilgrim Press, 2005).

Mark Yaconelli, *Contemplative Youth Ministry: Practicing the Presence of Jesus* (Zondervan/Youth Specialties, 2006).

Way to Live: Christian Practices for Teens, ed. Dorothy C. Bass and Don C. Richter (Upper Room Books, 2002).

Note: I'm indebted to Melanie Dobson-Hughes, my friend and fellow staffer at the Duke Youth Academy for Christian Formation, for sparking some of the ideas for the prayer, reflection, and "narrowing it down" activities in Part 1. We led a youth visioning retreat together for Asbury Temple UMC in Durham, N.C., in which she led us in similar practices.

TEMPLATE FOR SESSION SEVEN
Dreaming for Change, Part I

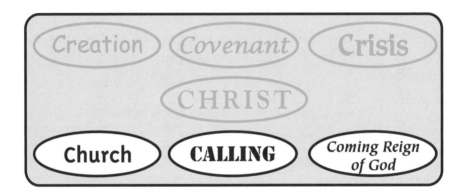

Newspaper Joys and Concerns (8–12 minutes)

Ahead of time, set out the newspapers, scissors, and tape. Create two large posters out of newsprint — one labeled "Joys" and one "Concerns" — and tape these on the wall.

As participants arrive, invite them to review the newspapers and cut out articles, images, or words about the local community that they find particularly uplifting, as well as those that they find particularly saddening or frightening (each participant can cut out multiple items). Have them tape what they've cut out to the appropriate posters on the wall, creating a group collage. As they work, invite them to talk informally about the high points and low points of their week.

Welcome (2–3 minutes)

Once most of the group has arrived, gather everyone together, welcome them, and say something like, "I've had us create these collages for a reason. For this session, I want us to keep our community at the forefronts of our minds. As a church, we are called to respond to its needs in some way. We don't just exist in a bubble. Jesus calls us to reach out to the world, to find Jesus *in* the world. So for the next two sessions, we're going to practice the Christian art of 'discernment,' or the art of figuring out what God wants us to do. In this session we're going to spend some time in prayer and discussion as a group in order to discern a particular problem in our community that we sense God wants our church to address."

> Christian discernment = the art of figuring out
> what God wants us to do

Opening prayer

Leader: The Lord be with you.

Group: And also with you.

Leader: Let us pray ... [say the following, or improvise your own variation]. Compassionate God, you know the joys and sufferings of the community that surrounds these walls; you know also the strengths and graces of our church. Give us eyes to see this community as you see it, wisdom to discern your will for responding to its needs, and courage as a church to answer your call — that your reign will be on earth as it is in heaven. Through Jesus Christ our Lord. Amen.

> Prayer begets faith, faith begets love, and love
> begets service on behalf of the poor.
>   — Mother Teresa of Calcutta

An Honest Look (10–15 minutes)

Return the group's attention to the collages on the wall. Starting with "Joys," invite those who wish to do so to briefly explain what articles, images, or words they chose and why. Do the same for "Concerns." Say, "Who would like to explain briefly what they chose and why?

Explanations should be short, and the rest of us will refrain from commenting, judging, or problem-solving."

> If your group is large, break into small groups for these explanations and then return to the larger group for discussion.

Once everyone has had the chance to speak, invite the group to discuss the following regarding the "Concerns" collage:

- Who is affected by the issues in this collage?
- What usually happens in response to these issues?

Prayer Exercise: Guided Imagery

(10–15 minutes or longer, as needed)

Say something like, "Part of what we've been doing is simply looking honestly at our community. Some of it is joyful and beautiful, some of it is difficult and sad. As Christians, we believe that God in Christ has deep compassion for the broken lives in our midst. God knows each of these people in the depths of their being (here you might name some of the people in the articles or point to pictures on the poster, slowly and thoughtfully). God knows every location, every situation. God even knows the stories that never get reported, the problems that people are too hurt or scared to name aloud.

"So right now we're going to attempt to see these situations from God's perspective, to feel the way God feels about them. We're going to do that by spending time praying in a special way known as guided imagery. The way it works is that we settle into a comfortable position, close our eyes, and spend some time in silence. Then I will invite you to imagine certain places, people, situations in our community, and how God might feel about those situations. There will be lots of silence in between the invitations, so be patient and focus on your prayer. The only thing I ask is that you keep your eyes closed and not distract your friends out of respect for our time with God. We will keep silence until the prayer time closes. When it's over, we will reflect on what we saw and sensed in the prayer. Questions?"

Take a few questions if needed, answer them briefly, but most of all ask participants to trust the process.

PRAYER WALK and PRAYER TOUR

Feel free to substitute other forms of prayer for the exercise in this section, such as a solo prayer walk around the neighborhood (in silence), or a prayer tour by car or van to schools, police stations, hospitals, neighborhoods (both upscale and struggling), homeless shelters, etc. At each location, have everyone stay in the vehicle. Pause for silent observation, and then ask "Lord, where are you working in this place?" Again, allow for prayerful silence for several minutes before moving on to the next location. Both the prayer walk and the prayer tour may take 30–60 minutes, so plan accordingly.

If desired, light a candle, or several. Invite participants to settle into a comfortable position — some may lie on the floor if they wish. If need be, separate those who might prove to be distracting. Invite participants to close their eyes and breathe slowly in and out. Allow a minute or two of silence as they breathe.

Then say something like, "I invite you to imagine that Jesus is leading us on a tour of our community. We follow him out the front door of this building [or our church] and head out into the neighborhood. What do you see first? [*Pause for a minute*] As you keep heading down the street, what else do you see? [*pause*] Now Jesus is taking us to the school with the best [or worst] reputation. What is going on there? [*pause*] Who do you see? [*pause*] In what ways are the people there thriving? [*pause*] In what ways are they broken and hurting, in need of healing and grace? [*pause*] Now imagine Jesus' response.

What is his facial expression? What does he say, if anything? What does he do? ... "

The prayer can continue in a similar way as you walk students through their community. Invite them to imaginatively visit neighborhoods with the best [or worst] reputations, the hospital, police station, jail, court house, homeless shelter, shopping centers, etc.

Desired result: Through prayer, to begin to recognize specific areas where God is concerned and acting for their community.

Close with something like, "Lord, we surrender all of these situations into your hands, trusting your Holy Spirit to work in the lives we have seen. In the name of the Father, and of the Son, and of the Holy Spirit. Amen."

Reflection / Creative Response (10–12 minutes)

In an atmosphere of quiet expectancy, gather the group back together. Distribute paper and colored markers. Invite participants to silently write or draw something about what they saw and how Jesus responded during their time of prayer. They can write in the form of key words, lists, phrases, a first-person essay, a letter, poetry, etc., or they can draw one large picture or several smaller images, a comic strip, a story board, etc. Encourage them to be creative but not to get so wrapped up in their work that they lose track of their prayer. You may wish to play some gentle instrumental music in the background as they work.

While the group is working, prepare five posters labeled "School," "Home," "Workplace," "Neighborhood," and "Institutions and Agencies." Tape these up on different walls, or at least spread them out from one another.

Highlights (10–15 minutes)

Say to the participants, "Now you will each be given 2 minutes to tell about what you saw, heard, or created during the time of prayer. Sharing is not compulsory, but encouraged. Nor is it for the purposes of feedback or problem-solving, but simply reporting. This is a time for witnessing to experiences with God in prayer." Break into small groups of three.

> The aim of discernment is, as Aristotle advocated, to have the right feelings at the right time — or ortho-pathos.
> — David F. White

Then bring the larger group back together and ask for highlights from each group. As they are reporting, you or the designated scribe should keep track of issues under the various poster headings — recognizing that certain themes or problems, such as racism, will carry across the columns. Try not to offer much commentary, and refrain from problem-solving. Before moving on to the next activity, discuss:

* What is missing from these columns, if anything? (If you notice that something like racism is absent — but you know this to be a problem in your community — say something like, "I wonder why racism isn't on here...." Don't fish for a response, but simply raise the issue. Invite others to phrase their comments in similar ways.)

Narrowing It Down (10–15 minutes)

Distribute at least one washable marker (watch for bleeding through the paper) or crayon to each participant. Again, in an attitude of prayer, and as gentle instrumental music plays in the background (optional), invite participants to review the issues listed on each poster. Have them put a check mark next to *three* issues they feel are most important — not three for each column, but three total. Encourage them not to let their friends' choices affect where they

> The poster labeled "Institutions and Agencies"
> could include such situations as lack of
> childcare facilities, overcrowded prisons,
> people with addiction in hospitals, overworked
> social workers, churches that serve only their
> members, etc.

put their marks, but to prayerfully reflect on the inward vision they saw and the creative response they put on paper. Participants are *not* to comment on their friends' choices. Also mention that if some issue or problem comes to mind that is not listed, they may write it in.

Ask a volunteer who is good at math to tally up the marks by each of the items, creating a master tally next to each item. Put a #1, #2, and #3 next to the items receiving the first, second, and third highest number of marks. Invite the group to step back and review the posters as a whole. Discuss highlights, using questions like these:

• What common themes do you see?

• In what ways are the top issues related?

• How do you feel about what we've identified here?

• How might God feel about what is identified here?

Summing Up (5–8 minutes)

Say something like, "Okay, we've done really good, prayerful work today. We've spent some time in God's presence, listening to God's heart for our community. We've spent some time reflecting creatively on what we've heard and seen. We've also spent time listening to one another and identifying some common themes. And finally, we've named key issues that we feel God is calling our church to address. Based on our poster work, the top three issues are [list them in order, starting with #3]. It's my sense that #1 is the priority at this point, although we will hang on to the others so they aren't forgotten.

#1 may not be your first choice, but in identifying these problems together, we're practicing something called consensus. That means each of us is willing to go along with the top choice for the sake of the larger group.

"What we've done today is the Christian practice of 'discernment.' [Here you may want to read or summarize some of the material from the 'Prepare Your Mind' section (page 97 above.) Discernment is what the Apostle Paul prayed for on behalf of the earliest churches. Listen to this. . . . [Here you can read either Philippians 1:9– 11 or Colossians 1:9–11 — or both of them — noting key words and phrases.] The goal is that we, as a church, will bring glory to God by dreaming as God dreams and bringing change to our hurting world. This isn't limited to the adults or the leaders in the church. *All* of us, by virtue of our baptisms into Christ, are part of that dreaming and acting.

"When we get together next time, we will take this one issue that we've identified and brainstorm concrete steps God might want us to take in response. In the meantime, please ask your parents, guardians, mentors, friends, pastor, and other church leaders to pray for this process. We are doing this on behalf of the whole church family, don't forget! So we need all the support we can get."

> Desired result: Through creative response, group reflection, and consensus, to identify one key concern that participants feel God is calling your church to address.

To close, invite the group to stand in a circle holding hands. As a closing benediction, you read aloud, or let a participant read aloud, Ephesians 1:17–23. Look around the circle as you read, emphasizing that this benediction is for *them*, for these youth, standing here. Close with, "Go in peace, in the name of the Father, and of the Son, and of the Holy Spirit. Amen."

Follow-up and Announcements

Announce the time and place of the next session.

Arrange for any emissaries that need to be sent to other church leaders or structures.

Leave the posters up on the walls for the next session.

Other ideas, suggestions:

• Using camera phones or digital cameras, invite the participants to go out into the community and take pictures of the things they see. Where do they see pain and brokenness? Where do they see signs that God might be up to something — signs of the in-breaking kingdom? Download the images into a computer and then show them as a slide show for a time of worship.

• To extend the discernment process to the broader congregation, invite pairs from your group to speak with the pastor or other key leaders, specifically asking for prayer. Or to make presentations to the missions/outreach team or committee of your church. Or to write up an announcement for the bulletin. E-mail parents and mentors about the discernment process, also asking for prayer.

Session 8

Dreaming for Change: Part II
Sarah Arthur

LEADER PREPARATION

For the "Leader Preparation" for Session 8, see the material for Session 7, beginning on page 96.

TEMPLATE FOR SESSION EIGHT
Dreaming for Change, Part II

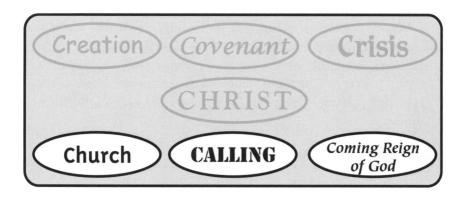

Invitation to Engagement (3–7 minutes)

As participants arrive, review the posters from the previous session of prayer and discernment. Ask informally questions like, "What have you been wondering since our last session? What do you feel God is doing with all this?"

Encourage the participants to bring up to speed people who are present now but were not at the previous session. Invite those people to join in at this point and go forward. Generally speaking, do not try to add new ideas at this point or go back and re-do the discernment.

Welcome (2–3 minutes)

Once most of the group has arrived, gather everyone together, welcome them, and say something like, "I'm so glad to be with you here. Well, it has pretty much always been the case that the church is facing decisions from within and from without. In this session, let's dig into examples from church history of Christians who responded in meaningful ways to problems facing their communities. We are called to the same task today."

Opening Prayer

Leader: The Lord be with you.

Group: And also with you.

Leader: Let us pray . . . [feel free to say the following, or improvise your own variation]. Merciful God, you know the joys and sufferings of the community that surrounds these walls. You also know the strengths and graces of our church. Give us eyes to see this community as you see it, wisdom to discern your will for responding to its needs, and courage as a church to answer your call. Through Jesus and by the power of your Holy Spirit. Amen.

Decisions, Decisions (8–14 minutes)

Create two columns on the board or poster paper, one labeled "Family/Household" and the other "Church." (Either you or one of the participants can be the "scribe" for keeping track of group discussion on the board.) To introduce this section say something like, "We all make decisions every day. Let's look at how decisions are made in our family or household."

Have each participant turn to a partner and discuss the following questions. Each person gets 2 minutes.

- How does my family/household usually make decisions? What are the steps in the process for us?

- How does it usually turn out?

- What are we doing well and what might we want to change about our decision-making process?

Then invite pairs to share highlights with the larger group while you or the designated scribe keeps track of responses in the column labeled "Family/Household." Sample steps for decision-making might include talking about the problem as a household, arguing, persuading, voting, seeking consensus, bribery, mutiny, adults making decisions for everyone else, individuals seeking advice from people other than family members, and prayer (we hope!).

The Church's Story (10–20 minutes)

Say something like, "We are not the first group of Christians to face challenges and decisions. Even in the 'family' that was the early church, not long after the Ascension of Jesus and the coming of the Holy Spirit at Pentecost, the new believers had to figure out how to respond to all kinds of problems that arose. The question is, how did they know what God wanted them to do? Let's look at three of those situations."

Break into small groups of three or four. Distribute Bibles to every participant (or small group), and assign each group one of the following passages: Acts 1:15–26; Acts 6:1–7; or Acts 15:6–22, 30–32 (be sure to tell this last group that the problem being debated is whether Gentile converts have to be circumcised like Jews in order to become Christians — since in the early church, Christianity was a "sect" within Judaism). If you have more than three groups, assign the same passage to more than one group. Have each small group select a person who will present their discoveries to the group. Have each group identify:

- The issue or problem facing the believers.

- The steps in the discernment process (what happens first, second, third, before they reach a decision).

- What is particularly "Christian" about their decision-making process (e.g., what Christian practices did they engage in? prayer, laying on of hands, etc.)?
- What is the result?

As you explain the group task write for all to see (a) issue, (b) steps, (c) how Christian, (d) result.

Bring the larger group together. Hear discoveries. Keep track of the steps in the process (including uniquely Christian practices) in the column labeled "Church." Sample steps include naming the problem aloud to the whole group (e.g., Peter in Acts 1:15); appealing to Scripture (Acts 1:20); brainstorming ideas and suggestions (Acts 1:23); prayer (Acts 1:24); casting lots (Acts 1:26); laying on of hands (Acts 6:6); debate (Acts 15:7); persuasion (Acts 15:10–11); silence (Acts 15:12); listening (Acts 15:12); consensus (Acts 15:22); and selecting the best option(s) (Acts 15:22).

Discussion

- What surprises you about the decision-making process of the early church?
- Where do you see similar steps in the way our church or youth group makes decisions today?
- What steps are missing in our current processes? Why do you think those practices have been lost?

Reflection
Our Story and the Church's Story (8–15 minutes)

Discuss:

- Considering the issue we identified last week and the model of the early church's decision-making process, what steps in the process have we already taken?
- What steps do we need to take yet? (Tip: allow time for exploring here.)
- Who is willing to help us move forward in taking those steps?

> Desired result: To discover ways the early church
> practiced Christian discernment.

Working Groups (12–20 minutes)

Divide up into groups of four or five based on interest (prayer, print communication, face-to-face communication with key leaders, networking with other ministries, etc.) and have groups brainstorm concrete steps for how the church can respond to the issue identified last week.

- Who do they need to involve in the process?
- What agencies or ministries already exist in the community that your church can partner with (or already partners with)?
- How will your group communicate with those ministries or agencies?
- What other steps must be taken?
- Who is willing to take those steps?

> The place God calls you to is the place where
> your deep gladness and the world's deep hunger
> meet. — Frederick Buechner

Bring everyone together. Write the Buechner quote for all to see. Let three volunteers take turns reading it aloud. Notice and point out the variations in emphasis. Say something like, "Christian discernment is discovering what God wants us to do. Sometimes we refer to this as a calling, or vocation. It is both individual and communal. How has or could our process in this session help you identify a 'place God calls you' "?

Bring groups back from the working groups to report on their discussion. Keep track of highlights on poster paper, including concrete steps to be taken and who take them. Identify any areas of overlap and ways you can streamline time and people-power. Set realistic, concrete deadlines (through consensus). Identify who will be responsible to do what, and who will help them be accountable to follow through.

> You may need to identify a task force, made up of members of this group who are especially passionate and gifted with regard to this issue. They can continue to meet and follow up on the project.

Summary (2–3 minutes)

Summarize for the group what they've done over the past two sessions. Refer to Alliterative C's, like Church, Calling, and the Coming Reign of God.

- How are we living into the Reign of God?

Liturgy for the Laying on of Hands (10–15 minutes)

Transition to a worshipful location or attitude. Stand or sit in a circle.

Lighting of the Candle.

Collect: Commissioning God, you love the broken and call your church to respond to the brokenness we see: grant that we may not rest until we have done your will, to the glory of your name. Amen.

Song: Sing a song about following God or God's will, such as "Seek Ye First" (*United Methodist Hymnal,* #405), or "Be Thou My Vision" (#451), or a similar hymn from your favorite songbook.

Laying on of Hands

Leader: In keeping with the practice of the early church, we invite those who have offered to take concrete steps in helping our church reach out to our community to please stand in the center of the circle so the group can lay hands on you and pray for you.

> *Those who are so called gather in the middle of the circle. Hands are laid on their shoulders or heads.*

Leader: May the Holy Spirit grant you wisdom and power to fulfill the tasks that are before you, for the sake of this church and our community. To the glory of God, through Christ our Lord.

All: Amen.

It is possible that all of the participants have agreed to perform some task or other, in which case you might invite them one at a time into the circle (if it's a smaller group and if you have time); or you can invite everyone to stay in a circle, but to place their right hand on the shoulder of the person next to them as a kind of "laying on of hands."

You may want those in the circle, or the group as a whole, to say a prayer together, such as the prayer entitled "For Courage to Do Justice" from the *United Methodist Hymnal* #456 or "Justice" from the *New Century Hymnal* #863 or a similar prayer from your denominational hymnal.

Closing Song: "In the Lord I'll Be Ever Thankful" (Taizé) or "Jesu, Jesu" (*United Methodist Hymnal* #432) or "Jesu, Jesu" from the *New Century Hymnal* #498 or a song your group knows about answering a call to serve Jesus in the world.

Benediction (based on Philippians 1:9–11):

> *May your love overflow more and more with knowledge and full insight, to help you determine what is best, so that in the day of Christ you may be pure and blameless, having produced the harvest of righteousness that comes through Jesus Christ, for the glory and praise of God. Amen.*

Follow-up and Announcements

• If you've identified a task force to continue addressing the issue the group has identified, further follow-up can happen with the rest of the group through, for example, the youth group or Sunday school classes.

• Invite participants to do some research on the Internet about Christian ministries in other communities, including Sojourners in Washington, D.C., The Simple Way in Philadelphia (the key spokesperson is Shane Claiborne, author of *The Irresistible Revolution* and *Jesus for President*); L'Arche communities in various cities (which reach out to the disabled under the leadership of Jean Vanier).

Part Three

TABLE

Session 9

Exploring Eucharist:
Stale Snack or Soul-filling Supper?

Fred P. Edie

LEADER PREPARATION

O taste and see that the LORD is good;
happy are those who take refuge in him.
— Psalm 34:8

Prepare Your Soul

Read Psalm 34:1–10

What are your deepest hungers?

_____

_____

_____

For inner peace?

_____

_____

_____

For reconciliation with neighbors?

_____

_____

_____

For righteousness?

_____

_____

_____

For restored creation?

_____

_____

_____

And what about your students? How are their own deepest passions being folded into the passion of God?

_____

_____

_____

Or where are those passions missing the mark, distorted, or domesticated?

_____

_____

_____

With these wonderings in your mind's eye, pause now to prayerfully imagine yourself together with all those persons you care about feasting at table with Jesus Christ, crucified and risen. Taste and see hunger satisfied, passions fulfilled.

Prepare Your Mind

Too often young people fail to eat and drink deeply at Christ's table. Such "failure to thrive" may be the result of negligent, ham-handed, or reductionist pastoral practice, but it may also stem from insufficiently cultivated theological imagination. Thus, this session proposes to do two things: (1) invite students to imagine deeply the power and meaning embodied in communal meal sharing; and (2) consider the theological breadth of Eucharist (also known as "Holy Communion" or "Lord's Supper.")

Each time we sit down to eat a meal together we are invited into God's activity in the world. The food we eat is a gift of God's good creation. Its abundance invites our thanksgiving for it and for those who steward it from field to table. When we have food we may be moved to share with those who do not, and so our eating becomes a microcosm for the working out of God's justice as well. Food also implies sacrifice — plants, animals, and even soil-dwelling insects and microbes die in order that we may eat — so part of eating thankfully is recognizing its cost. Meal-sharing is always enhanced by the generous and thoughtful hospitality of the host — seating arranged to ensure rich conversation, table elegantly (or simply) adorned. Persons so blessed by this sort of hospitality may find themselves sharing stories or commemorating important events, and, in the process, being woven into new or reconciled communities of friendship. Not least is the delight good food offers. Its rich tastes, aromas, and textures provide more than mere caloric input. As surely as it renews our bodies, sharing in a good meal renews soul, mind, and heart.

The description above already rings with Eucharistic overtones. However, this session will also invite students to move from the imaginative and the sensual to the theological. It will invite students to explore how all of the theological Alliterative C's are embedded within the church's meal at Christ's table. Obviously, the central holy things of Eucharist, bread and drink, are created things that imply at once *creation's* goodness (Psalm 34:8) and the willingness of God to be made incarnate through ordinary material reality. Further, as Jesus says, "this . . . new *covenant* in my blood" (Luke 22:20, 1 Corinthians 11:25) binds us to him and to one another throughout time. *Christ's* sacrificial death (1 Corinthians 5:7; Hebrews 9:26) *and* resurrection life (Luke 24:30–31) are made apparent in this meal. Those who eat at Christ's table are made into one body, the *church* (1 Corinthians 10:17). The church is *called* to participate in God's transformation of the world, in part, by sharing its food with those who are hungry (1 Corinthians 11:20–21). In this manner it partly embodies God's *Coming Reign* in which all are invited and find a place at Christ's table (Luke 14:12–14), even to share in communion with the saints (Hebrews 12:1).

The session seeks to display the theological breadth of Eucharist and not to get hung up on thorny issues like the degree of Christ's bodily or spiritual presence or absence in the meal. As with the session on baptism, however, leaders (and students) may benefit from recalling the importance of *anamnesis* (translated "remembrance" in 1 Corinthians 11:24) and *prolepsis* to the church. *Anamnesis* intends "re-membering" or "re-presenting" of God's saving events — including centrally the life, death, and resurrection of Jesus Christ.

> **Considering Eucharist as flat memorial is inadequate at best.**

Prolepsis means "future-presenting," that is, realizing God's promised End powerfully (if only partially) in the present Eucharistic moment. From a biblical perspective, therefore, considering Eucharist as flat memorial is inadequate at best. The biblical witness is to God's graceful, if mystical, past, present, and future action in and through the Eucharist.

> **Taking and taking and taking Eucharist has begun to make me believe that something happens there.**
> — Duke Youth Academy for Christian Formation, participant (2009)

Prepare Your Heart

Consider how, in your own experience or that of your congregation, participation in Eucharist has been either an indifferent matter, a practice at the very center of your Christian life, or possibly one that became an acquired taste over time. Your group may also bring a variety of attitudes to the subject, ranging from hostility to indifference to hunger. Be cognizant of how young people of today are more aware of food and food culture than in past generations. Perhaps the best attitude of your own heart in preparing to teach this session is that of an angel bearing gifts rather than an anxious defender of theological orthodoxy. The session invites deep imagining more than it intends to instruct persons exactly on what they should think or do. In fact, you may invite students to prepare their own hearts by putting away cynicism and preconceived ideas about Eucharist and, instead, opening themselves to new leadings of the Holy Spirit.

> **What happens at the Lord's Table?**
> **God's grace-full past, present, and future!**

Prepare Your Space

If you do the "Welcome Participants to a Feast" activity (page 128), gather and prepare the food and table ahead of time. Arrange the tablecloth and other touches (serving dishes, candles) to signal that this food is somehow more than the usual doughnuts and juice. Place the table near the teaching space in the room. If your tradition allows, you may use this same table (perhaps tidied up a bit and less cluttered) for the celebration of Eucharist at the conclusion of the session.

Organize seating so that students may easily divide into pairs and work in small groups and also so that the entire group may focus attention on you and a marker board or other writing surface.

Prepare Your Supplies

* Bibles.
* Marker board or newsprint and appropriate marker.
* For the "Welcome Participants to a Feast" activity (page 128) here are some suggestions: assortments of freshly baked breads; honey; different grape juices; grapes; cheese; milk.
* Cloth for the table.
* Plates, cups, napkins. If accessible: samples of fine china, tableware, drinking glasses plus serving bowls, pitchers, and serving utensils.

Prepare Your Plan

If you do the "Welcome Participants to a Feast" activity (page 128) and there are other adults in the classroom, ask them to serve arriving students from the table with the foods that the students wish to sample. Adults should convey hospitality to the students (as will the fine food carefully laid out) and the gentle expectation that they are to eat with a certain amount of decorum as the group gathers. Good-natured comments like "Let's try not to be Cretans" and "Savor it" can help convey your expectations for gratitude and enjoyment of this meal that is more than the usual snack.

For "Explore the Theological Breadth of Eucharist" you will need to prepare handouts with individualized instructions for small groups (see page 132).

For "Celebrate Eucharist" (see page 133) you will need to arrange ahead of time for a clerical presider or ordained clergyperson if your tradition requires such. (Note that some traditions do not offer Eucharist to a subset of the wider congregation.) Invite a leader who cares about the quality of Eucharistic celebration. Traditions vary on where the meal may be observed. If it is not a moveable feast (from your sanctuary to your classroom, for example) you will need to ensure availability of that space and travel time for your students. Ask the celebrant if she or he wishes that you gather the elements.

Where time is short you may skip "Welcome Participants to a Feast," "Option for Continued Discussion," "Celebrate Eucharist," or all of these.

Where time is abundant, in addition to using all the activities, you may choose to turn the individual small group assignments in "Explore the Theological Breadth of Eucharist" into assignments for every small group to tackle. Even more ambitious, these small group assignments could become the basis of learning stations. In this model the small groups rotate through all seven of the "theological Alliterative C" stations. In addition to the bare minimum of assignments for investigating Scripture and responding to the questions, stations would also be decorated with artwork, food, or symbols inviting further reflection. Relevant texts from your tradition's Eucharistic liturgy or hymns that develop a particular Eucharistic theological theme could also be placed in stations. Whereas 10 minutes are designated for small group research in the regular session, using learning stations will require approximately 70 minutes (seven stations at 10 minutes each, with groups rotating through all seven stations). Plan accordingly.

> This suggested activity could be a follow-up session or part of a mini-retreat. What if it occurred the same day or week that your congregation celebrates Eucharist?

Prepare Your Publicity

Publicize this event with a blurb like this: "Come enjoy a rich banquet of food as we study and reflect on the (Eucharist/Holy Communion/ Lord's Supper *or insert your community's word here*). Taste and see that the Lord is good!"

Prepare in Prayer

Loving God, whose Reign is made known through a feast to which all are invited and through which all are filled: Grant that our group may grow to eat and drink more deeply the life and death of Jesus Christ. I ask this in the name of the One who feeds us abundantly. Amen.

Prepare Further

For more biblical and theological investigation into Eucharist see E. Byron Anderson, editor, *Worship Matters* (vol. 1); Laurence Hull Stookey, *Eucharist: Christ's Feast with the Church*; or Alexander Schmemann, *For the Life of the World: Sacraments and Orthodoxy*.

For the formational power of ritual symbols see Browning and Reed, *The Sacraments in Religious Education and Liturgy* (Parts I, II, and chapter 9), and Fred Edie, *Book, Bath, Table, and Time* (chapters 2, 3).

TEMPLATE FOR SESSION NINE
Exploring Eucharist:
Stale Snack or Soul-filling Supper?

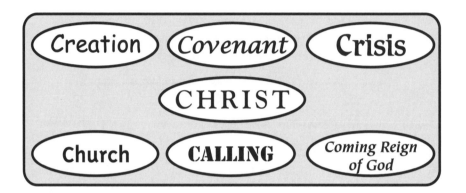

Key Scripture: Psalm 34:8

> O taste and see that the LORD is good;
> happy are those who take refuge in him.

Objectives

- To invite participants to imagine deeply the power and meaning embodied in communal meal sharing.
- To consider the theological breadth of Eucharist (also known as "Holy Communion" or "Lord's Supper").

Appetizer / Opener:
Welcome Participants to a Feast

(5–10 minutes prior, as participants arrive)

Ahead of time prepare a "banquet table" as described at the beginning of "Prepare Your Space" (page 125) and "Prepare Your Plan" (page 126), using the types of supplies listed in "Prepare Your Supplies" (page 125).

The foods need not be exactly those listed under "Prepare Your Supplies," but a simple rule of thumb is the less processed the foods are the better. (The suggested foods all have historical relationships to the Eucharistic meal.) Prepare the table artfully to display the goodness of the various foods. Leaders should arrive early enough to both set the table and serve the participants from it as they arrive. Invite participants to enjoy the meal with one another and to eat thoughtfully since the eating is part of their learning.

Opening Prayer (1–2 minutes)

Leader: The Lord be with you.

Group: And also with you.

Leader: Let us pray. Life-giving God, you feed us with the good things of your creation and the holy things of [Eucharist, Holy Communion, Lord's Supper — use your community's language throughout]. Move us to feast gratefully today and every time we gather at your table. We pray through Jesus Christ in the power of the Holy Spirit. Amen.

First Course:

Telling Stories of Memorable Meals (5–10 minutes)

Say: "Our session today is intended as a general re-introduction to the Eucharist. It invites you to do two things. One is to re-imagine why meal sharing in community (including sharing in the Eucharist) may be for us such a rich blessing. The second is to reflect on what Eucharist means, for there are many delicious flavors of theological meaning that our Eucharistic celebration enacts.

"As you continue to eat together, I'd like you to gather in pairs and to respond to this prompt: 'Describe to one another an enjoyable and memorable meal in which you have participated. Include in your descriptions the foods, those who dined with you, the setting, the occasion, the hospitality offered, and so on.' "

To model this, you could briefly share your own story of Christmas or Thanksgiving dinner or some other memorable meal.

Monitor your clock and occasionally remind conversation groups how much time remains.

Reflecting on the Key "Ingredients" of Memorable Meals (12–30 minutes)

As storytelling and time wind down, ask participants to direct their attention back to you. Pose this question to the entire group: "In light of the stories you told one another, what are the *ingredients* of enjoyable and memorable meals?"

Here you invite public responses and record them on marker board or newsprint. Responses will likely fall out along these lines:

• *Food* — delicious, fresh, simple or elegant, aromatic, artfully prepared, beautiful, abundant, appropriate to the occasion or context

• *Occasion* — unique, seasonal, or annual, commemorating or celebrating, marking a life passage; reconciliation

• *Ritual and Symbol* — grace first, toasts, procession of courses, stories shared (and embellished), candles lit, songs sung, manners expected, customs followed, guests on best behavior

• *Diners* — longtime friends, family, or other loved ones, strangers who become friends, multiple generations, hungry! delighting in food and one another, telling stories, sharing laughter or sorrow

• *Hospitality* — host's preparation creates beautiful welcoming setting, gifts of generosity and good food invite intimacy and deepened community, host anticipates the needs of the guest, host often offers her or his best (china, silver, drinking goblets, linens, recipes, foods — though "best" varies from place to place)

• *Results* — Full! gratitude, deepened relationships, solidified community, deepened identity as family, friends, or members of a group, anticipation for the next gathering

The above list is not exhaustive. Participants will undoubtedly offer profound insights not included in it. You should encourage students to say more when you sense they are on the cusp of something more. You may use the list to prompt a neglected line of thought or to help deepen students' initial insights. The point is to awaken students to meal sharing as a blessed gift of human existence and to the dynamics contributing to this gift.

Say: "We've begun with sharing good food and describing what makes meal sharing a gift to our lives. [*Point to the list*] Now I'd like you to think about our church's practice of Eucharist. Where in the words spoken at Eucharist, or in the gestures, or in the ritual symbols, or in the actions of the host and guests do you see similar dynamics at work?"

Desired result: To awaken participants to the blessed gift of meal sharing.

Answers to this question may not only prompt analogical thinking ("We say grace at both our table and the Eucharistic table," or "Eucharist makes us more solid as a Christian family"). It may also raise further critical questions from students ("How is the Eucharist both like and *unlike* a regular meal?") or questions of the adequacy of Eucharistic performance (Why does a pastor always seem in such a hurry at the table? Why is everybody just going through the motions?) Any one of these responses may elicit further profitable discussion so long as time allows and you have the willingness to entertain them.

Summary statement: "Whatever we may think about Eucharist at present, it is essential to understand that everything we can say about the richness and blessedness of sharing good food in community is also part of our Eucharistic participation. Eucharist is *more and less* than an ordinary meal, but it is a meal. Re-imagining how meals may bless and even transform us is one step in receiving Eucharistic food with deepened gratitude."

How is Holy Communion both more and less than an ordinary meal?

Option for Continued Discussion (10–15 minutes)

Question: If the summary statement on the previous page is true, what does it suggest about how we should celebrate Eucharist in worship?

(Possible answers to be recorded on the board: Eucharist should look more like a meal, we shouldn't skip "grace," bread and drink should look more like food, host should be expectant and happy, we should be grateful, nobody's in a hurry, Eucharist should emphasize community over eating alone, etc.)

• What would be required to implement these changes?

• What can *we* do about that?

• What more do we need to learn first?

Second Course:

Explore the Theological Breadth of Eucharist
(15–30 minutes)

Write on the marker board the list of Alliterative C's: Creation, Covenant, Crisis, Christ, Church, Calling, Coming Reign of God. See above Session 6 on baptism (particularly page 91) to briefly convey each of these theological categories to the students. For more on the Alliterative C's, see also pp. 119–20 in *Book, Bath, Table, and Time* by Fred P. Edie (Pilgrim Press).

> Desired result: To explore connections between Eucharist and major themes of our Christian faith.

Divide the group into seven small groups (or, if the group is large, multiples of seven) to investigate Eucharist in light of each of the theological categories. Consider designating a student as facilitator for each group. Assign adults to the small groups if they are available. Distribute the handouts you prepared ahead of time, one to each group (handouts are on pages 222–228).

After allowing approximately 10 minutes for small group biblical research and responses to questions, call the small groups back together for sharing. Focus the sharing with this question: "How did you discover your theological theme to be related to or embedded within the practice of Eucharist? That is, how is your theme a part of Eucharist?" Allow all groups to respond, collecting their insights on the board as they report. Next ask:

• Which of these themes are new to your understanding of Eucharist? Which are familiar?

• Which of these themes are most evident in our congregation's Eucharistic practice?

• Which are muted or absent? What could be done about this?

• How will what we have discussed cause you to engage Eucharist differently in the future?

Eucharist: it's food for life!

Final Course:
Celebrate Eucharist (12–18 minutes)

If feasible, culminate this session by sharing in the worshipful celebration of Eucharist together. To the extent your tradition allows, ask the clerical leader to actively involve students in the liturgy. Possibilities include having them offer the Eucharistic gifts, helping to prepare the table, playing and singing the congregational responses in the Prayer of Great Thanksgiving, and assisting with the distribution of bread and drink.

Eating Well: Food, Justice, and Eucharist

Meredith Stewart

LEADER PREPARATION

Prepare Your Soul

Scripture

> By awesome deeds you answer us with deliverance,
>   O God of our salvation;
> you are the hope of all the ends of the earth
>   and of the farthest seas. . . .
> You visit the earth and water it,
>   you greatly enrich it;
> the river of God is full of water;
>   you provide the people with grain,
>   for so you have prepared it.
> You water its furrows abundantly,
>   settling its ridges,
> softening it with showers,
>   and blessing its growth.
> You crown the year with your bounty;
>   your wagon tracks overflow with richness.
>   —Psalm 65:5, 9–11

Story

My great-grandmother was the kind of woman who spent an entire morning preparing the noonday meal. When she died, she left a pantry full of foods that she had canned the previous summer. Every so often we would open a jar and enjoy the results of her labor. Even though there was nothing special about them, those beans seemed to taste better than other beans. Eating them was sharing in her memory.

Questions

• What did you have for your most recent meal?

_____

_____

_____

• What do you know about where the foods that made up that meal came from?

_____

_____

_____

• Consider Psalm 65:5, 9–11. What words connect you and your food to the Creator?

_____

_____

_____

Prayer

> *Creator God, thank you for the abundance of your creation. Forgive us when we fail to take good care of it. Help us to be good stewards of the fertile soil that you have given us. Amen.*

Prepare Your Mind

In a culture where fast food has become a norm, it is not often that we sit down and think about the origins of the food we eat. Eating has lost some of its sacramental character as we are increasingly encouraged to do more. Youth are especially likely to eat hurried meals on their way from school to sports practice or dance class.

When we become forgetful about the source of our nutrition, we lose the richness of the experience of table fellowship and the narrative of Scripture. The Bible is teeming with agricultural metaphors.

Jesus speaks of the kingdom as being like a sower who sows seeds on different types of soil. However, unless we come from a farming community or have experience growing or harvesting our own food, the value of these metaphors may be lost on us.

> Desired result: To help participants make connections between the act of eating and the sharing of Christ's body and blood in the Eucharist.

There is increasing awareness of the importance of conservation and of the dangers of overuse of the earth. However, these concerns are not always articulated as theological concerns. This session seeks to help youth make connections between the act of eating and the sharing of Christ's body and blood in the Eucharist.

Taking greater care to consider where our food comes from and to pray for and work to improve the conditions of those who grow and produce our food leads us to a greater appreciation of God's creation and our responsibility to be stewards of it.

Prepare Your Heart

It's so easy to see eating as a utilitarian act. We eat to keep ourselves alive. Often we engage in eating almost mindlessly. We take for granted that there will be food in the grocery store for us to buy and that a great deal of the preparation of that food will have already taken place. Despite this attitude, great meals we remember were often ones that we or our loved ones were intimately engaged in preparing. The celebration of the Eucharist or the Lord's Supper reminds us of the importance of bread and grapes — things from the earth.

Prepare Your Space

You could plan to have this session outside if the weather is agreeable and there is a suitable space for your group without significant distractions. If you are not able to have the session outside, try to find a location that allows natural light or a view of the outdoors. If you plan to use a PowerPoint type slide show, set up the projector, screen, and chairs so that everyone will be able to see the presentation. Arranging the chairs in a half circle will allow everyone to see not only the screen but also one another, and thereby allow for conversation.

Prepare Your Supplies

- A small pot or pots (or small paper cups).
- A seedling or seeds.
- A computer (with PowerPoint or another program you can use to show a slide presentation) and a projector, or a series of photos illustrating stages of food production and distribution, or paper and markers.
- Candles and matches.
- Food to eat together such as fresh fruit, vegetables, and dip.
- The Elements (bread and wine or grape juice according to your tradition) and other necessary items to celebrate the Eucharist.
- A clergyperson as needed for Eucharist.

Prepare Your Plan: Overview and Strategies

Consider how you form small groups, where you will eat, and where you will worship (will it include Eucharist?). Will you go high tech or no tech?

Prepare Your Publicity

Use the quotation on page 143 from the co-president of Whole Foods in your announcements, e-mails, bulletin blurbs, etc.

All week, ask people, "What do you think Eucharist has to do with food?" Then invite them to attend or pray for this session!

Prepare in Prayer

Lord, I am thankful for the opportunity to be a part of the lives of the young people in our group. Guide me as I lead them in exploring your creation and the ways in which we can work toward a more just society. I pray:

For those in the youth group who are in any trouble or distress...

For the friends of those youth in our group...

For those of the church who work with youth...

Prepare Further

Wendell Berry, *The Art of the Commonplace*, ed. Norman Wirzba (Shoemaker and Hoard, 2002).

Fred P. Edie, *Book, Bath, Table, and Time* (Pilgrim Press, 2007), especially chapter 2.

Norman Wirzba, *The Essential Agrarian Reader: The Future of Culture, Community, and the Land* (Shoemaker and Hoard, 2004).

TEMPLATE FOR SESSION TEN
Eating Well: Food, Justice, and Eucharist

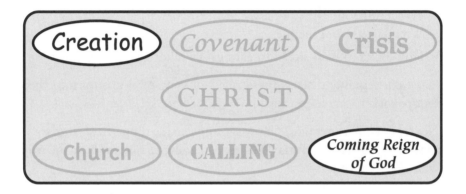

Key Scripture: Genesis 2:15

The LORD God took the man and put him in the garden of Eden to till it and keep it.

Objectives

- To understand eating as both a means of sustaining the body and a way to be good stewards of the earth.
- To make connections between the act of eating and the sharing of Eucharist.

Prayer (1–2 minutes)

Let a participant or leader either offer this prayer or create one with similar themes.

Heavenly Father, we thank you for the gift of the good earth and the fruits of it. Forgive us for taking for granted our food and those who labor to bring it to us. Bless those hands that have nurtured our food, carried our food, and prepared our food. May the food we share be a foretaste of the heavenly banquet we will all share. Amen.

Appetizer (5–10 minutes)

Say: Describe a typical meal for you or your family. Ask one another detailed questions, such as:

- What is the mood of the meal?
- Who prepares the meal?
- Who cleans up afterward?
- What is a typical menu?
- How much time is given to eating? To talking?

Have participants discuss these questions in small groups and then report back to the larger group.

Next, say something like, "How we approach eating affects our souls as well as our bodies. Today we are also going to discuss how the way we eat affects others."

Digging into Scripture (8–12 minutes)

Invite the group to turn to Genesis 2:8–10, 15 and 3:17–19 and read the passage.

Say something like, "Nudge your neighbor and tell a story (actual or imagined) of you or someone you know working in a garden or on a farm. You will have 2 minutes each (4 minutes for your pair)."

Now lead a discussion, using questions like these:
- When you think of working in a garden or on a farm, does it seem like easy or hard work? Why?
- Why does God put the man (Adam) in the Garden of Eden? (*Guide the group toward Genesis 2:15 if they need help.*)
- After Adam and Eve disobeyed God by eating of the tree of the knowledge of good and evil (see Genesis 2:16–17), what does God say about the ground in Genesis 3:17–19? (*For example, it will be cursed, it will be difficult for man to grow food.*)
- How do you think the curse is different from God's command in Genesis 2:15? (Before they disobeyed, do you think the work of growing food was not difficult for the man and the woman?)

Where Does It Come From? (8–12 minutes)

Ask the group to imagine the hands through which the food that they eat passes. Ask,

- Who is directly involved with the food we eat?

As the participants name each of these types of laborers, have a visual depiction of this kind of worker. You could either find pictures on the Internet and print them out or create a PowerPoint visual presentation or let volunteers draw sketches.

- Those who work in the field (tilling the soil, planting the crop, watering the crop)
- Those who harvest the food
- Those who clean and pack the food
- Those who transport the food
- Those who stock the food in stores
- Those who sell the food

Ask:

- When you sit down to eat a meal, how often do you think of the people that we mentioned who were involved in bringing your food to you? Why?
- Why is it easy to forget these people?

Digging into Scripture (5–8 minutes)

Say something like, "Remembering that our food comes from the ground reminds us that we are not in charge of our own lives."

Introduce the next Bible passage by saying something like, "In this passage, God has given instructions to Jeremiah to give to the Israelites who are living in captivity in Babylon. Let's all look at Jeremiah 29, verses 4 and 7." Ask:

- Why were the Israelites told to plant gardens and eat what they produced?

- Why might the Israelites not want to plant gardens in Babylon? (They wanted to think about getting back to Jerusalem as soon as they could; planting gardens meant they were going to have to stay in Babylon for some time.)
- How could planting gardens be a sign of hope?

Pop Quiz (4–7 minutes)_____

Give the group the following quiz. Allow the participants to make guesses before you reveal the answers.

- Out of every dollar spent on food at a grocery store, how much money goes to the farmer? (*27 cents*)
- How many miles does the average food item travel from the field to our mouths? (*1,500 miles*)
- How many pounds of food does the average American consume each year? (*1,500 pounds*)
- What is the average hourly wage for an agricultural worker in the United States? (*$9.27. That's less than half of the average wage for all workers of $20.32. That's $19,280 a year for farmworkers and laborers, crop, nursery, and greenhouse workers, compared to the average of $42,270 for all workers.*

Source: U.S. Department of Labor, Bureau of Labor Statistics
www.bls.gov/oes/2008/may/oes_nat.htm#b45-0000

- How many farms are there in the United States? (*2,204,792*)

_____

Discuss the results of the quiz. Begin with questions like

- What answers were surprising to you?
- What did you learn that you had not known before?
- How do you feel about these realities?
- What might God's justice look like to these people?
- How can we be better caretakers of the land God has entrusted to us?

Digging Deeper into Scripture (5–8 minutes)

Prepare for the passage. Say, "the passage we are about to read takes place after Jesus' resurrection. Some of the disciples have heard the Good News of Jesus' resurrection but some have yet to hear. Jesus appears to two disciples who are walking along the road to Emmaus, a village outside of Jerusalem. They do not know who Jesus is. Jesus begins talking with them and explaining the Scriptures that spoke of the coming Messiah. Our passage picks up right after the disciples have invited Jesus to eat with them and Jesus has accepted their invitation."

How much do tomato pickers in Immokalee, Florida, earn? According to the *Washington Post* (April 28, 2009), "Workers are paid 45 cents for each 32-pound bucket, the same wage as thirty years ago."

"In the long term, how can something be sustainable if it doesn't include the welfare of those who produce it?"
— Walter Robb, co-president of Whole Foods

Ask a participant to read Luke 24:29–35. Then ask:

• If the two disciples didn't know who the stranger was, why do you think the disciples asked Jesus to share a meal with them?

• When did the disciples first realize that Jesus was the one who was eating with them?

Say something like, "In the Eucharist, we share in Christ's body and blood. That body and blood are found in the form of bread and wine. In the meal of the Lord's Supper, we all share food. The everyday food of bread and grapes becomes out of the ordinary when we share the Eucharistic meal."

Discuss other insights and questions from participants.

Life Grow (3–10 minutes)

Ask the group:

• How could you become more aware of where your food comes from? (Examples: Read food labels, visit a farmers' market and talk with those who are selling produce, ask the grocer.)

• How could we work with God for justice concerning food laborers and the distribution of food?

• How are you going to live in new ways in relation to Genesis 2:15?

Suggest that one way to take care of God's earth is to grow one's own food. If feasible, have the group plant herbs that can later be used in cooking. There are several possible options for the planting. You might use seeds or a seedling (which could be purchased from a farmers' market or a home and garden store). If there is space in the church yard or a sunny spot in your meeting room you could put the plants there. You might also have a plant for each member of the group to take home and care for. Herbs that work well include basil and spearmint.

Still Hungry? (5–10 minutes)

Let a volunteer read aloud this quoted passage from *Book, Bath, Table, and Time* by Fred Edie. Elicit and discuss reactions:

> "The church once understood its ritual meal as the multivalent enactment of multiple biblical stories including, centrally, Jesus' sacrificial self-giving and resurrection presence. Not only does table enact the book's central story, however; it is essential for lived understanding of it."
> — From *Book, Bath, Table, and Time*, page 112

+ How is the Eucharistic table essential for living the central story of the Bible?

Bonus Activity

Investigate the growing movement of community gardening. One example is the Anathoth Garden planted in Cedar Grove, North Carolina. After a significant event rocked the community, people began to come together to build bridges by growing food. You might be amazed by what God has done! Their Internet address is: *www.anathothgarden.org.* You could either gather this information prior to the session and present it for discussion or assign an interested participant (or pair) to investigate and report back.

> Perhaps your youth will be inspired to join or begin a community garden. There's nothing quite like growing food with God!

Preparation for Worship

Before worship assign several students to read alternating verses from Psalm 65:5–14.

If you are able, move to a space that is inviting for worship. This might be an outdoor area such as a garden or a chapel or nave. If you are limited to a classroom space, gather the chairs in a semicircle. Have a few candles and a basket of fruit or vegetables as a focal point.

Worship (7–25 minutes; length will vary depending on whether Eucharist is celebrated)

Have previously assigned students read Psalm 65:5–14 aloud.

Invite the group to join in singing a hymn of thanksgiving for the goodness of the earth such as "This Is My Father's World" or "For the Beauty of the Earth." Or you might use a song that speaks to Eucharistic themes such as "One Bread, One Body" or "Taste and See."

Say: "Let's express to God our feelings upon hearing the Word from Psalm 65."

Sharing the Eucharist during your worship service could be a powerful, tangible reminder of the connection between food that comes from the earth and the food of Christ's body and blood that we share at the Eucharistic table. If you are able, invite a pastor or priest to be present at the gathering so that the Eucharist may be celebrated.

For an offering, why not let participants donate money to purchase food for persons who are hungry?

Whether Eucharist is celebrated here or not, conclude the session with table fellowship and eating of the bounty of God's earth. Provide food that is easily identifiable as freshly grown, such as whole fruit or sliced vegetables with dip.

Follow-up Activities and Announcements

If your church takes an offering (either of money or bread and wine for the Eucharist) to the front of the church during worship, you might suggest that this offering include food to be taken to the local food pantry or a shelter. While many churches collect food for the poor, incorporating this collection into worship is a reminder of the centrality of food to our common life and underscores the connection of Eucharist to the sharing of food.

Hospitality Meal: Breaking Bread Together

Laurea Glusman McAllister

LEADER PREPARATION

Prepare Your Soul

Begin your preparation by reading Mark 14:1–25. In the constant rhythm of activity in our daily lives, we may fail to remember to prepare a space in which to receive our God. By Christ's own instruction, the disciples went ahead and prepared the space in which to enjoy table fellowship with Jesus. When we take the time to prepare a meal, to prepare the space in which we enjoy that meal, and then enjoy that meal in leisurely fashion with both those who are within our own communities and those who are new to us, we encounter the triune God in powerful ways. Our God is a God of relationship, who calls us to nurture our relationships with one another. Sharing Christian hospitality with the stranger opens our hearts and minds to relationship with all of God's precious children. Consider the ways that you take time to prepare to receive Christ in your own life, and how you receive those whom you encounter in your daily life.

What's one thing you do to welcome someone to a meal?

_____

_____

_____

In the accounts of Jesus at table in Mark 14:1–25, to which guest do you feel an affinity, receiving Jesus' hospitality?

_____

_____

_____

How might you make your presence more hospitable to the stranger?

_____

_____

_____

How might you be changed and transformed if you open yourself to such experiences?

_____

_____

_____

Prepare Your Mind

Think about the last church supper that you attended with youth present. A typical scenario shows the youth sitting at separate tables, enjoying conversation that might seem like Greek to the adults around them and, generally, experiencing segregation from the rest of the community. The teens rush to the front of the food line, "wolf" down their food in under 10 minutes, and disappear to play a game of basketball before youth Bible study begins.

Now consider what meals may look like in the homes of some of your young people. Breakfast is a cereal bar grabbed on the way out the door to school. Lunch is eaten in haste in a 25-minute lunch break, during which many students have to eat, go to their lockers, use the restroom, and perhaps even meet with a teacher or attend a student council meeting. An afterschool snack is consumed on the way to sports practice or music lessons, and dinner is kept warm in the oven, to be eaten in front of the television whenever it is convenient for the young person. Of course, some families still enjoy dinner together around the table, but the prevalent scenario in many homes is that meals have become merely functional. Their sole purpose is to provide energy so that all, young and old alike, may perform the many activities in which they are involved. The modern meal is often a far cry from what Christ envisioned when he instructed his disciples to go ahead of him and prepare the table so that he might enjoy his last meal with them.

The early church had a sense of what Christ was calling his people to experience and learn by sharing a common meal. The love feasts that preceded the act of Holy Communion reenacted the sharing of food, drink, conversation, and relationship at the Eucharistic table. For youth today, the connection between Eucharist and the common meal has been too often lost. They have little experience of lingering over food, of cultivating skills for meaningful conversation, or of deepening relationships through the sharing of a meal. When we begin to relearn the art of Christian hospitality, by lovingly preparing the space for a meal, sharing food with one another, and learning to connect with one another through meaningful conversation, the meaning of Holy Communion is renewed. As Christ shared hospitality with his disciples at the Last Supper, and as his disciples shared hospitality with him by preparing the room, we are called to do similarly.

> **Desired result: In following Christ's lead of hospitality, to get a foretaste of the heavenly banquet that awaits.**

This session will teach young people the art of lovingly preparing the space for a meal and of sharing that meal with people new to them; in doing so, they will encounter the triune God who calls us into deep and meaningful relationship with one another. It is hoped that such an experience will cause them to take pause, to reconsider their understanding of the gift of food in God's creation, its purpose and role in our lives, and its ability to provide more than physical sustenance. Moreover, it is hoped that in following Christ's lead of hospitality, they will get a foretaste of the heavenly banquet that awaits them when God's reign is ushered in.

Prepare Your Heart

What adjectives describe the typical mealtime experience in your home?

_____

_____

_____

Where do teens in your group typically eat? How are relationships being fostered or hindered there?

_____

_____

_____

Who in your church exhibits the gift of Christian hospitality? How might you involve them in this event?

_____

_____

_____

How are nutrition and flavor important to Christian table hospitality?

_____

_____

_____

Describe a time you felt really welcome at a meal. What made it meaningful?

_____

_____

_____

In what ways is eating together a foretaste of heaven?

_____

_____

_____

Reflect on This Eucharistic Prayer

> *By your Spirit make us one with Christ, one with each other, and one in ministry to all the world, until Christ comes in final victory, and we feast at his heavenly banquet.*
>
> *— United Methodist Hymnal,* p. 10

How does this happen at a holy meal?

_____

_____

_____

Is it also glimpsed at a common meal? How?

_____

_____

_____

Prepare Your Space

Prepare a space with enough tables and chairs to seat both your youth group and a group that you will invite for dinner. In order to facilitate conversation and relationship building, separate tables with spaces for eight to ten are preferable to long tables that seat everyone. Comfortable lighting and temperature convey hospitality, as do decorations, signs, table coverings, and place settings.

Prepare Your Supplies

- White butcher paper.

- Crepe paper or other streamers.

- Matches and votive candles or tea lights.

- Confetti.

- Something for centerpieces (for example, flowers or glass bowls with clear marbles and floating candles).

- Colored paper or card stock (to make cards for tables).

- Markers.

- Scissors.
- Real plates (glass or china), flatware and glasses for everyone participating.
- Three or four serving dishes for each table.
- Napkins.
- Adhesive nametags.

Hint: Set a tone by using permanent plates and glasses, not disposables.

Prepare Your Plan

Invite to dinner a group that your group would not normally interact with for a meal. The group that you invite might include another generation in the church, such as a class of older adults, or a youth group from a church of a different racial or socioeconomic makeup. Involve participants ahead of time in discussing whom to invite and extending the actual invitation. Ask the visiting group to prepare a simple meal to share with your group. Explain that they will prepare the meal and bring it with them and that your own youth will prepare the space and then serve the meal and clean up afterward. It is recommended that you show or explain this session to the leader of the visiting group, so that the purpose of the activity will be clear to everyone participating. Also, attend to the hospitality of providing options for those with special dietary needs.

Involve participants ahead of time in discussing whom to invite and extending the actual invitation.

Meal suggestions

- Mediterranean: Tabouli, hummus, pita bread, stuffed grape leaves, dried apricots, nuts, grape juice

- Soft tacos: black beans and rice, meat, cheese, tomatoes, salsa, lettuce, sour cream, guacamole, chips, tortillas

- Lasagna: lasagna with meat, vegetarian if desired, green leaf lettuce salad, dressing, garlic bread

Tip: Part of the idea behind asking the visiting group to prepare food is the hope that the menu itself will invite conversation about the tastes and life experiences of the guests. An ideal meal would be familiar and authentic to those preparing it, as well as palatable to all who will receive it.

Prepare Your Publicity

- Prepare posters and flyers entitled "Who's Coming to Dinner?" with details of the event.

- Distribute the flyers to potential attendees. Wouldn't this be a good time to invite again that kid who has faded away?

- Put a blurb in the church newsletter. Send a copy to the pastor or priest and the church council, vestry, or board.

Tip: Why not provide flyers or other written invitations for the leader of the guest group to distribute to her flock?

Prepare in Prayer

Holy Jesus Christ, God in the flesh, your life embodied the hospitable reception of others. Transform my life so that I too may embody the humble and kind reception of others. Teach me to share myself with your people, as you shared yourself with us. Guide me in sharing the experience of a holy meal with these young people; let their lives be transformed by you, so that they experience your holy presence as they linger over food, drink, and conversation with others. Amen.

Prepare Further

Use a Bible dictionary or online resources to familiarize yourself with the role of hospitality in the Middle Eastern cultures of Jesus' time and our own.

See also session 13 on Sabbath for connections to hospitality and meals.

Fred P. Edie, *Book, Bath, Table, and Time.* Cleveland: Pilgrim Press, 2007, especially chapter 2.

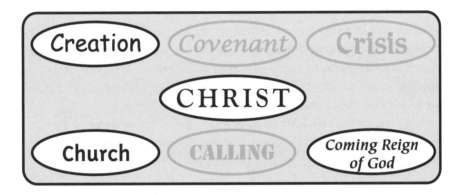

Key Scripture: Mark 14:12–16

On the first day of Unleavened Bread, when the Passover lamb is sacrificed, his disciples said to him, "Where do you want us to go and make the preparations for you to eat the Passover?" So he sent two of his disciples, saying to them, "Go into the city, and a man carrying a jar of water will meet you; follow him, and wherever he enters, say to the owner of the house, 'The Teacher asks, Where is my guest room where I may eat the Passover with my disciples?' He will show you a large room upstairs, furnished and ready. Make preparations for us there." So the disciples set out and went to the city, and found everything as he had told them; and they prepared the Passover meal.

Objectives

- To share Christian hospitality with strangers.
- To help young people make the connection between the hospitality of a shared meal and the hospitality of the Eucharistic table.
- To teach young people the value of taking time to slow down, linger over a meal, and enjoy Christian fellowship at a meal.

Overview

The youth group will spend time preparing a space in which to share a meal with another group and then share the meal while learning about different biblical characters who embody hospitality.

Welcome (3–10 minutes)

Gather participants and tell them that today they are going to learn about Christian hospitality. Say something like, "Part of living out our Christian faith in our daily lives is the offering of hospitality to others, as well as learning to receive hospitality. What do you think of when you hear the word, 'hospitality?' "

You might want to list their answers on a large sheet of butcher paper. Using either a dictionary or the definition given here written on a card, ask one participant to read the definition aloud:

Hospitality: the general or cordial reception of guests; offering a pleasant and sustaining environment; a pleasant reception or disposition when receiving others; being open and receptive to new ideas; the sharing of one's space, belongings, and time in order to show kindness to others

After the group has added their own thoughts and definitions of the word, say something like, "We see many examples of hospitality in the Bible: in the way that Jesus received and interacted with all different kinds of people; in the way that he shared every aspect of his life with his disciples, including his meals; and in the carrying on of that shared life by his community of followers.

Today, we are going to share Christian hospitality with others. We have invited the [*insert name of group you invited*] to enjoy a meal with us. We will show them hospitality by spending time setting up for the meal, decorating the room, making our space for the meal feel comfortable, welcoming them into our youth community, and serving the meal. We will also *receive* hospitality as we eat the meal that they have prepared for us and share in fellowship with them at the table."

Prayer (2–5 minutes)

Holy God, in our busy and hurried lives, we may too rarely take the time to share the joy of fellowship at the table. In his instructions to the disciples just before he shared his last meal with them, and in his sharing of that meal as an act that he instructed his followers to continue to carry out as a practice, our Lord taught us that the preparation for and sharing of a meal together is a vital way in which to experience your holy presence. May your Holy Spirit work through our hands as we take time today to experience you through the giving and receiving of hospitality among your children. Amen.

> How many of your youth group regularly gather around the dinner table with their families? Would your youth group like to take time to enjoy home-cooked meals together in each other's homes?

What Makes a Meal Good? (5–12 minutes)

Invite the youth to think about the different elements of a good meal that make it enjoyable. (If you have done this in Session 9, you can bring this list back out to remind them; see page 130.) The goal is to get them to think about more than the food or conversation, but to help them think about the atmosphere, the reception of one's guests, and what makes a meal hospitable. Say something like, "One part of enjoying a good meal together is the preparation of the food. What are some other aspects of a good meal that make it enjoyable?" (Again, you might want to write out their responses on a large piece of paper.)

After they have made the list, say something like, "We are going to divide into groups to prepare to receive the [*insert invited group name*] and share the meal with them. Our goal is to include many of the elements of a good meal that you have listed here."

Get Volunteer Groups Ready

(5–10 minutes to explain and form the groups)

Depending on the number of participants, you can divide them into groups. Suggestions for groups include:

Servers

This group will receive the food from the guests when they arrive and put it into family-style serving bowls. Each table should have one server assigned to bring food to the table once the meal has begun, to make sure that each table has what it needs and generally to attend to the needs of the table. The meal is served family style, with large bowls of food and pitchers of drink that the guests pass around the table. Ask the servers to get a bowl of each item for their table and then sit with their table to eat. You should have as many tables as you need to seat your invited guests and your youth group and one server for each table.

Table Setters

- Use real dishes (as opposed to paper plates), silverware, and glasses if you have access to them. You might ask some parents to lend you these items for the session.
- Set each place with a fork, knife, spoon, plate, and glass.

Decorators

Invite this group to use their creativity to decorate the space. Suggested decorations:

- White butcher paper on the tables that can be decorated with crayons, or some other type of tablecloth.
- Crepe paper or other streamers.
- Votive candles.
- Confetti on tables.
- Glass bowls with water (you can put clear marbles in the bottom and add a floating candle).
- Welcome banners made from white butcher paper.

Biblical Characters

Label each table with a biblical character that embodies hospitality. Either print the story of each biblical character on a card on the table, or make sure each table has a Bible, so that the diners may look up their characters. Then make cards with that biblical character on them for each seat at the table. Shuffle the cards from all of the tables, in order to mix up the groups during the meal (see "Greeting Your Guests" just below). Suggestions for characters to use: Ruth; the woman who bathed Jesus' feet with perfume on her hair; the apostles on the road to Emmaus; the Shummanite woman and Elisha.

> Hint: Provide adhesive nametags either at the
> door or at each seat.

Greeting Your Guests

Have some greeters at the door to receive the guests as they arrive. Instruct them to greet each person by introducing themselves, asking the guest their name, handing them a card with a character, and inviting the guest to take a seat at the table marked with that biblical character. (Your youth should also take cards, so that they are dispersed among your invited guests rather than sitting all together.)

Setup (8–20 minutes)

Now assemble into groups and tell them how long they'll have to prepare. Let them get to work.

> Tip: You could designate a student in each group
> to be a leader. You could also have an adult
> or two for each group to facilitate cooperative
> progress.

Enjoy the Meal (as long as possible, 45–60 minutes)

Allow time afterward for reflection, clean-up, and follow-up.

Once the guests have arrived, ask everyone to take their seats. Say something like, "We want to welcome you to dinner tonight. We are thrilled to have the opportunity to spend this time with you, and we appreciate your willingness to share hospitality with us. Each table is labeled with a model of hospitality from Scripture. I invite you to learn about these examples, and think about how we might model our own lives after theirs. Please relax and take your time. Enjoy the meal, and afterward we will spend some time reflecting on this experience together."

Tip: You are encouraged to ask a young person to give this introduction.

Reflection (12–22 minutes)

Depending on the size of your group, you may want each table to reflect separately, or you may want to lead the entire group in reflection. You may also choose to do some reflection with your invited guests, and then do further reflection after your guests have departed.

Suggestions for Reflection Questions

1. What does it mean to be hospitable?
2. What are some ways that Christ practiced hospitality?
3. How did each group here tonight practice hospitality?
4. Was there anything that was difficult about practicing hospitality?
5. What contributed to your feeling comfortable or uncomfortable?
6. What did you learn in this encounter that you wouldn't have learned otherwise?
7. How might this change the way you see people who seem different from you?

8. Can you see any connection between what we experienced here and what we experience at the communion table?

9. What could it mean to live out Christian hospitality in your everyday life?

Worship

◆ You may choose to move into a short service of Holy Communion after the meal. Arrange this ahead of time as needed with your clergyperson. Provide for needed elements, tableware, vestments, etc.

◆ Alternatively, gather the two groups into a circle and ask them to hold hands. Light a candle in the center of the circle, and sing a simple song about communion such as "Let Us Break Bread Together," "Take a Little Bread," or another short song familiar to your group.

> *Prayer: Holy God, you gather us as one community tonight so that in sharing a meal together we may understand better what awaits us in the heavenly banquet. Teach us to show hospitality to everyone we encounter in our daily lives, give us patience to love those around us as Jesus modeled for us, and help us to take the time to encounter each other in meaningful ways, so that we may encounter you. In your holy name we pray. Amen.*

Alternatives

• The idea behind the guests preparing the meal is that Christian hospitality is both given and received by both groups. However, if the invited guests are not able to prepare the meal, you might ask parents to prepare a meal for the whole group. We suggest inviting these parents to share the meal with your youth group and invited guests, so that all who serve also share in the banquet.

• Another option for the preparation of the meal is to have some of the group come early to cook. Just make sure that everyone in the group participates in some part of either preparing the meal or the space.

• In case the groups need help with conversation, add mixer questions to the table, once they have learned about their biblical character. Examples: What's the worst trip you've ever been on? What's the best trip you've ever been on? What's one of your favorite meal memories? If you could live and eat in another nation, where would that be?

Part Four

TIME

Session 12

Learning to Keep God's Time: Christian Worship as Time Travel

Fred P. Edie

LEADER PREPARATION

Prepare Your Soul

Dorothy Bass, author of *Receiving the Day,* says that time is a gift from God. So characterized, time may not be earned, spent, squeezed, stretched, or lost. It may only be received gratefully from the Giver of all good gifts. What's more, according to Bass, as with all divine blessings, time is given to us in abundance. Each of us receives all the time we require to be and do what God intends. There is no lack of time! Bass's theology of time is at once beautiful and at odds with the ways we often live our lives. We consider time short, frenzied, and fleeting. In response, we seek to buy time and at all costs not to lose time. A moment spent in idleness rather than productivity may lead to . . . we dare not go there. Yet go there we must if we wish to confront the demons of frenzy and boredom and learn how to receive God's graceful gift of time.

Read Genesis 1:5. How does the passage of time haunt you?

_____

_____

_____

Bless you?

_____

_____

_____

What would it take for you to receive more of the latter and less of the former?

_____

_____

_____

Prepare Your Mind

Human societies have always patterned time in order to understand themselves and the meaning of their own existence. In the ancient world these patterns were tuned to nature. There was day time, night time, summer time, and winter time, plus times for planting and harvesting. Unsurprisingly, human societies with organic understandings of time also imagined themselves to be part of the rhythms of the cosmos and subject to powers greater than themselves.

For much of its history, the church participated in these rhythms but also bent them to its own distinctive purposes. The morning bells of the village church chimed in the day that the Lord (not the sun) had made. Other occasions for prayer throughout the rest of the day were closely tied to events of Jesus' last day: his conviction, crucifixion, death, and burial. On Sundays these bells tolled out the astounding news of Christ's resurrection as they summoned the community to worship.

During the industrial revolution, however, church bells gradually gave way to massive clocks in public squares. This new means of patterning time also signaled a radical shift in human self-understanding. Time became mechanized, "kept" by a machine constructed by its human masters. The clock tower also exerted social control, "telling" workers when their shifts began or when they could rest. Further still, time no longer stopped at sunset. Mechanized time continued through the night as did the demand for industrial labor.

A symbol of still another evolution in time is the digital wristwatch. No longer does time sweep by with the movement of large (if mechanized) "hands"; instead it pulses in beams of light. Such a device makes far more difficult imagining time's passage; we are left with disjointed, disconnected fleeting fragments of time. Adding to that fragmentation, time now belongs to individuals. I keep my time and you keep yours — each on our own wrists. Or, with the advent of PDAs and smart phones, my personal time keeps me on the relentless treadmill that is my schedule.

The most recent (and most bewildering) construal of time comes to us courtesy of Albert Einstein. Delighting in playing with mind pictures, Einstein imagined himself riding away from the village clock tower on a beam of light. He reasoned that while time continued to pass "normally" for him, subsequent light beams registering the passage of time on the clock tower could never catch up to him, thus implying that time back home had stopped. Could time be variable? Einstein was, of course, conjuring relativity, and his scientific work has caused contemporary cultures to radically re-imagine a world that is postfoundational and, therefore, postmodern.

This brief passage through the history of time does not intend to advocate any particular version of time. Truth is, many of us live in all of these patterns of time simultaneously. It does invite us to recognize, however, that time is partly a human construct and partly beyond our meddling. Recognizing that we cannot, despite our best efforts, fully control time may save us from all kinds of idolatries — from eugenics to texting while driving. Recognizing that we inevitably vest time with meaning invites us to consider which meanings and which patterns of time connect us with God's redemptive purposes for the world and which do not.

Like other human communities the church also patterns time. And as with its other ritual symbols, the church's patterning of time is rooted in the worshiping traditions of Israel. God's people were known, of course, for their week — six days of labor and the seventh day reserved as a Sabbath before God. Keeping time in this way literally enacted them into their deepest storied convictions about God and themselves. God (the One of the busy six days) is *Creator* of all that is; God must also be *deliverer*, however, because a people still under pharaoh's thumb would get no Sabbath rest; and God *sustains* Israel in the present until the Messiah comes. A Sabbath commitment to complete cessation of labor signals that this community is dependent on God's providential care, not its own devices.

The early church adopted Israel's week, for the story it enacted was the church's story too; but soon the early church juxtaposed to the rhythm of labor and Sabbath rest its own worship on Sunday. Significantly, this day was also called the Lord's Day or the Day of Resurrection. The effect of this juxtaposition was the enactment of the church's own distinctive theological convictions for the centrality of Jesus Christ including, crucially, his resurrection from the dead. This resurrection event, to which the church witnessed, did not dissolve Israel's week; indeed it would be impossible to make sense of it without the week. Yet neither could the old week contain the enormity of this new thing. Indeed, the church's Lord's Day also came to be called the "eighth day" and the "first day of the new creation." In other words, Jesus Christ recapitulates all that the seven days mean but he also means more: Jesus is *messiah come,* Jesus is *God's Reign inaugurated,* Jesus is the *firstborn* of the *new creation.* The church accomplishes this witness to its revelation by juxtaposing to Israel's week its own worship on the Day of Resurrection. It's patterning of time witnesses to Jesus Christ.

> We mostly manage to turn the time God offers as gift into a relentless taskmaster. We scurry through our lives; we even hustle to prepare a teaching session on the gift of time!

As with the week, so it is with the high holy days. Next to Israel's yearly Passover festival the church soon juxtaposed its own Paschal celebration of Christ's passion and resurrection. And next to Israel's Pentecost commemoration of receiving the Torah came the church's celebration of the gift of the Holy Spirit. To Israel's lamb of the Passover is juxtaposed "Christ our Passover, sacrificed for us." Similarly, Spirit is juxtaposed to Law. Just as the writers of Scripture were inspired to use the stories, images, and meanings of Israel's Bible when crafting what came to be called the New Testament, so the church readily appropriated temporal patterns from Israel but made them "speak" a new "word" — Jesus Christ crucified and resurrected for the redemption of all creation.

What is at stake in the present patterning of time for the formation of Christian identity? First, congregations should be concerned for whose time they are keeping. Does the church calendar witness centrally to Father, Son, and Holy Spirit or to mothers, fathers, patriots, and turkeys? Does its annual round enact fully the birth, ministry, death, and resurrection, ascension, and crowning of Jesus Christ as cosmic king along with its hope for his future return, or does it settle for "Happy Easter" and "Merry Month-long Christmas?" Second, even in communities whose worship seeks to enact faithfully God's time, do participants in that worship understand the nature of this pattern? Can they articulate what it means and how it shapes their own lives? Do they see in it God's unfolding Story of Salvation? These are the issues that this session on the Christian patterning of time seeks to open to your students.

> **With respect to God's gift of time, most of us seem guilty of ingratitude at best and self-idolatry at worst.**

Questions

- Whose time are we keeping?
- How does that shape our lives?
- How could the church calendar point to God's unfolding Story of Salvation?

Prepare Your Heart

Perhaps any conversation about time in twenty-first century North America should begin with confession. We mostly manage to turn the time God offers as gift into a relentless taskmaster. We scurry through our lives; we even hustle to prepare a teaching session on the gift of time! We are impatient and bored with anything that requires more than an instant of our limited attention. Because we have created this sort of world for them, our young people maintain an equally frenetic pace. They multitask through the day, aspiring to achieve more than is humanly possible.

Prepare Your Space

If you choose to create calendars you will need sufficient table or floor space for groups to do their work.

Prepare Your Supplies

- General: board and writing tool, Bibles.
- Optional: hymnals or lyrics, accompanist or recording and playback device.
- For "Which Calendar Do You Keep" a resource describing the days and seasons of the Christian year may be downloaded ahead of time at *www.calvin.edu/worship/planning/insights/11.php*.

Groups may also wish to refer to Christian year "pie charts" available for download at Google images. An excellent poster of the Christian Year is available for purchase at *www.catholicsupply.com/BOOKS/annualbks.html*. (*Note:* this resource may include information about saints, which you can interpret according to your denomination's outlook.)

If you choose to fashion calendars in this session you also will need to provide newsprint paper, tape, and markers or crayons.

For "Consider the Meanings of Time" you may need to download the four images of the symbols ahead of time if you are not comfortable sketching them yourself. Find them at Google images.

Prepare Your Plan

Look over the session and decide how to allot the time. Decide which additional resources you will use (such as visuals) and display them prominently.

Prepare Your Publicity

How can you invite someone new to this session? Newspaper, e-mail, phone call, sign or banner on the street?

In your communications before this event, use catchy phrases like these or create your own:

- What *time* is it to God?
- How is worship like time travel? Come explore on [*date*] at [*time*] at [*location*].
- Why does the Christian year begin about a month *before* Christmas?

Prepare in Prayer

O God, giver of all good gifts, I give you thanks for the gift of time. Though you are beyond time, you blessed and fulfilled time by entering into it through none other than our Lord Jesus Christ. By your Spirit, help me to live as if time belongs to you alone and to receive each day with gratitude and hopeful expectation. Amen.

Prepare Further

Dorothy Bass's *Receiving the Day: Christian Practices for Opening the Gift of Time* (Jossey-Bass, 2000) is a wonderfully honest, yet hopeful and practical account of overscheduled Christians learning to live gratefully in God's good time.

Gordon Lathrop's *Holy Things: A Liturgical Theology* (Fortress, 1993) and Alexander Schmemann's *Introduction to Liturgical Theology* (St. Vladimir's Seminary Press, 2003) probe deeply into the church's patterning of time as a grace-filled means to enact its theological convictions and to witness to its central revelation — Jesus Christ is Lord.

Still another helpful resource is Robert E. Webber's *Ancient-Future Time: Forming Spirituality through the Christian Year* (Baker Books, 2004.)

Laurence Stookey's *Calendar: Christ's Time for the Church* (Abingdon, 1996) offers a detailed account of the origins of the Christian Year and the theological significance of time.

TEMPLATE FOR SESSION TWELVE
Learning to Keep God's Time:
Christian Worship as Time Travel

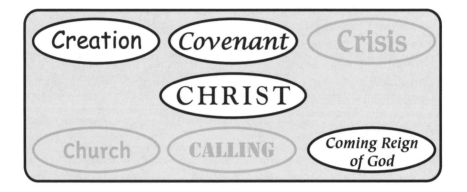

Key Scriptures: Genesis 1:5; Matthew 28:1

God called the light Day, and the darkness he called Night. And there was evening and there was morning, the first day.

After the Sabbath, as the first day of the week was dawning, Mary Magdalene and the other Mary went to see the tomb.

Objectives

- To consider the power of different patterns of time to shape participants' understandings of themselves and their world.

- To investigate how the Christian Pattern of Time most fully enacted in worship bears theological significance.

- To reflect on how the Christian Pattern of Time may become a gift to assist in reevaluating the past and living hopefully into the future.

Appetizer
Which Calendar Do You Keep? (7–15 minutes)

Say something like, "Humans mark time in a variety of ways. The rising of the sun marks a day. The ringing of a school bell can begin or end a school day. There are calendars for the school year, the fiscal year, the greeting card year, the agricultural year, the automotive year, the lunar year, and the Christian year. In small groups, create a poster depicting such a calendar. You may choose one that has been mentioned or offer your own ideas."

Pass out large sheets of newsprint paper and make markers or crayons available. When calendars are complete have the group post them on a wall or board next to one another where they may be seen by all.

Have a representative from each working group briefly describe their creative process and comment on the content of their calendar. When all have shared, ask:

+ Where do you notice points of overlap on these calendars? Why is this so?

+ Where do the calendars seem distinct or perhaps even in conflict with one another?

+ Is there a deep rhythm that your calendar marks or attends to?

+ Which calendar(s) do you follow? Rank them by the power they exert over the shape of your time.

+ What does this ranking suggest to you about how you are formed through the patterning of time?

+ Are you satisfied with this patterning of time in your own life? Why or why not?

Consider the Meanings of Time (12–20 minutes)

Say: "In this exercise I will invite you to reflect upon different symbols of time and time-keeping as a means to discover how they have shaped understandings of time. We'll also look at the self-understandings of human communities in relation to time. This sounds complicated, but just go with me and I believe you will see that it isn't really."

Show the following items or draw representative images one at a time. Allow for discussion of each before proceeding to the next one:

1. Sun dial

2. Village square clock tower

3. Flashing digital wrist watch

4. Albert Einstein streaking away from a village square clock tower on a beam of light (this one may require some explaining)

Any actual items you can display will add to the impact of this session. Might you have such a watch to show, or a miniature clock tower in your holiday decorations or in a child's toy chest?

After displaying an item or image ask these questions:

1. What does this image of time imply about how time has been understood?

2. What does this image of time imply about how human beings understood *themselves* in relation to time?

Note: You may wish to review the section in "Prepare Your Mind" (page 166) that discusses these images and their meanings in order to help facilitate this conversation. Below find possible responses:

Sun Dial

1. Time is tuned to cosmic, especially solar rhythms; divided into day and night and annual round; time sweeps by in a slow steady motion during the day then "stops" at night; time is cyclical, repetitive.

2. Human beings are embedded in these cosmic rhythms; humans are subject to powers beyond themselves (sun, moon, climate); people must cooperate with these powers in order to live; look to past to understand and anticipate future.

Village Square Clock Tower

1. Time becomes mechanized, more precise; extends past dark; never stops; becomes more scarce; begins to have value as a commodity.

2. Human clock builders become time's masters; mechanism of time increasingly exerts social control over persons' lives (advent of shift work); time is public, communal (one clock for entire village); mechanized time fits with Deist mechanized view of the universe and God as cosmic clockmaker who sets creation in motion but allows it to run on its own; diminished sense of time as an expression of powers that transcend human power or ingenuity; time is money.

Flashing Digital Wrist Watch

1. Time is fragmented into individual seconds or milliseconds; loses continuity with past and future (no more passing shadow or sweeping hands); places emphasis on the immediate, instantaneous now; symptomatic of transition to digital culture.

2. Loss of sense of importance of history as anticipation of future; focus on the now; time belongs to individuals with resulting loss of social bonds; time worn on the wrist eventually becomes internalized (the "ticking biological clock"); time seems to grow more scarce as means to keep it become more precise.

Albert Einstein

1. Time linked to energy; time may be bent, warped, sped up, slowed down;

2. Imagining time travel; appreciation for the vastness of cosmos threatens to diminish human significance in it; "The past is not dead. In fact, it's not even past" (Faulkner).

The Origins of the Christian Pattern of Time (with Help from Scripture and the Writings of the Early Church Fathers) (20–40 minutes)

Consider obtaining something like "Year of Grace 2011 Liturgical Calendar Poster" for your group. The calendar may be found online at *www.catholicsupply.com/BOOKS/annualbks.html.*

Other church year graphics can be found at Google, Church Year, images. The exercise seeks to locate the church's theologizing in the ways the origins of its time were juxtaposed to Israel's time.

This exercise invites students to consider the theological significance of the Christian Pattern of Time. Thus, rather than simply familiarizing them with a church year pie chart, it invites them especially to consider the development of the Christian Pattern of Time in light of Israel's time keeping. Seeing how church time is at once continuous with and dependent upon Israel's time and also radically discontinuous with that time may not only help students reevaluate Christianity's indebtedness to Israel but also see how Christian theology spoke a new word in an old temporal language.

If you have plenty of time, provide copies of the handout "The Origins of the Christian Pattern of Time" to your students (The five page handout can be found on pages 229–233). While students are reading the document, display the poster or graphic (pie chart) of the Church Year if you secured one ahead of time. In an extended session you could divide into small groups to research the biblical passages in the first three sections of the handout or assign persons individual passages. Allow an extra 30 minutes if you choose to assign and report on this research.

If you have less time you may choose to read or summarize the handout contents (or have students do this.)

Follow up with these discussion questions. They can also be found on page 234.

◆ Read Genesis 1:5, Genesis 2:2, and Exodus 20:8–11. What evidence do the Scriptures contain pointing to the origins of the Christian Pattern of Time?

- Much of the Christian Year developed fully only after the era of the church of the New Testament. How should Christians evaluate the Christian Pattern of Time in light of this fact? For example, is the Christian Pattern of Time faithful to the Gospels or does it detract from or distort them?

- What seems to be the relationship between Jewish and Christian calendars? How does this relationship impact your thinking about your own Christian faith?

- What does the Christian Pattern of Time suggest about the relationship between theological beliefs we know in our heads and convictions we carry in our bodies? Is one way of knowing more authentic, more truthful than the other?

- How attentive is our congregation to the Christian Patterning of Time?

- Which holy days or seasons seem to be emphasized? Which are diminished or left out entirely? To what effect?

- What can we do about it?

Christian Worship as Time Travel (10–25 minutes)

Say: "This exercise invites you to consider how Christian worship bends and stretches time in powerful ways. Allow me to mention two terms: "Anamnesis" and "Prolepsis" (write these on the board).

Anamnesis

Say: "Anamnesis" is a Greek word meaning the opposite of amnesia. *Anamnesis* means literally "the drawing near of memory") (see Stookey, *Calendar: Christ's Time for the Church* [Abingdon, 1996] 29.) To understand anamnesis better, consider the differences between these pairs of terms: remember and re-member; represent and re-present (write these on the board as well). In each case the meaning of *anamnesis* is more like the hyphenated term in the pairings. Ask:

- What are the differences in the paired terms? (*hyphenated terms are active and present-oriented with respect to considering what is past; non-hyphenated terms are passive and imply that the past is past*).

• Scholars say that Christian worship is characterized by *anamnesis*. What does this characterization imply about events marked by the Christian patterning of time? (*These events are somehow made present to our experience or we to them.*)

Elevate the engagement of memory and musical learners by singing together or hearing recordings of these songs.

Say: "Consider these lines from some Christian hymns":

"Yea, Lord, we greet thee, born *this* happy morning..." from "O Come All Ye Faithful"

"O sacred head *now* wounded..."

"Christ the Lord is risen *today*..."

Ask:

• How does our singing of these hymns participate in the dynamic of *anamnesis?*

• What does it mean to you that God's past saving actions are made present to our experience in worship?

• How might the dynamic affect the way we imagine or enact the future?

Prolepsis

Write the second term on the board: "Prolepsis."

Say: "This is an English word derived from Greek. It means 'to take something into our experience...ahead of the time at which it actually occurs.' With respect to worship it means 'bringing God's future into our present'" (Stookey, *Calendar*, 32). Ask:

- What kind of future is made present in worship? (*Delight in joining with saints in the heavenly vocation of praising God; the experience of Christ's resurrection, the same resurrection that is promised to all at the fullness of time; God's Reign of justice and peace as when all are welcomed to Christ's Eucharistic table as a "foretaste of glory divine"*)
- How may encountering God's future shape your own future?
- How do you want to live into God's future this week?

Prayer (3–15 minutes)

Transition from teaching and learning to praying. Use music if it helps.

Invite participants to a time of prayer, either in silence or speaking aloud voluntarily. They could form a circle or kneel in a chapel.

> Tip: Write or post the prayer prompts for all to see.

- God of the Ages, thank you for what I've learned here, such as...
- God of the Present, help me to...
- God of the Future, help me trust that...

Optional Follow-up: Use questions like these to assist participants in continued reflection and integration. Chat about them in the parking lot, in the dugout, or in cyberspace.

- What difference does it make whether the church follows the school calendar, greeting card calendar, or Christian calendar?
- What does it mean for God to enter time?
- Do you experience time more as blessing or as burden?
- How do you want to alter your approach to "time management" based on the discoveries of this session?

Session 13

Entering into Sabbath Rest

Sarah Kerr

LEADER PREPARATION

Prepare Your Soul

"Remember the Sabbath day and keep it holy." — Exodus 20:8

"On the seventh day you shall rest..." — Exodus 23:12

When we're tired, we might say that we need a little "R and R," meaning "Rest and Recreation." This definition is not far off from God's prescription for what God's creatures need, but God's formula comes differently and with the force of a command: God says to "Rest and Remember." First, God calls the people of Israel to rest. The word in Hebrew for "Sabbath" is *shabbat,* which literally means to cease or to rest. God called the Israelites to stop all their work every seventh day, even their efforts to find sustenance in the desert. For the Israelites, obeying this command while wandering in the desert meant risking great peril. To stop looking for food and simply sit in their tents seemed sheer folly in the middle of the wilderness. However, God gave them manna to eat, supplying their need while they received God's gift of *rest.*

Meanwhile, as they rested, the Israelites spent a day recalling God's marvelous acts on their behalf. This was the second command God gave them: to *remember.* The Israelites stopped their work so that they could focus on recalling the two great acts God had accomplished on their behalf: creation and exodus. After spending six days creating everything on earth and in heaven, God's grand finale on the seventh day was, of all things, to rest. However, God did not rest out of exhaustion; nor did God's rest mean relinquishing control and letting things "play out" in creation on their own. Rather, God rested because the creation was not only good but complete. It meant that the Creator of all things would now take on the role of the "King of the Universe," as the Jewish Sabbath prayers emphasize. The Israelites were able to rest in the desert because by doing so they remembered the God who rested, the One who created the world and continues to sustain it.

The command to keep Sabbath while living in the wilderness points out the need for creation to rest from our labors. It challenges us to face our presumptions of autonomy and self-sufficiency; it exposes our radical dependency. We are reminded that we are frail beings, who are dependent on the self-giving of the natural world and of other humans. This can be a terrifying reminder; often we would prefer to avoid it by keeping up our busyness and holding such a reminder at bay. However, while Sabbath calls us to remember that we are creatures, it also sustains us by reminding us that we belong to the Creator and King, who rested on the seventh day, who sent manna from heaven in the wilderness, and who calls us to rest in God's rule and provision. Resting is possible when we also remember the God who was satisfied with creation and took up his rule as the King of creation. Yes, we are required to stop and remember that God was satisfied with all creation.

How may we join God in this satisfaction?

_____

_____

_____

How may we trust that God would provide for us if we rested from all of our efforts? When might we secretly think that we really have to provide for ourselves?

_____

_____

_____

What variety or practice of *resting* is (or could be) good for your soul?

_____

_____

_____

What tendencies do you have toward not *remembering* God's provision?

_____

_____

_____

Pray over Exodus 20:8–11. Talk to God or jot down your prayer here about your own practices of resting and remembering God's provision.

_____

_____

_____

Prepare Your Mind

What Is Sabbath All About?

AS we have seen, the word for Sabbath in Hebrew is *shabbat,* which means "to rest" or "to cease." The Sabbath calls us to remember our three most basic relationships: relation with God, with creation, and with others. In Exodus 20:8–11, when God gives the command to "remember the Sabbath day and keep it holy," the reasoning is based on God's day of rest at the end of creation. God called the people of Israel to cease their work and remember that God both declared creation good and rested. Surely if the Creator was satisfied with the work and considered it complete, then God's people should also pause from their work and recognize the sufficiency and goodness of what God has done.

Which Day Is the Sabbath?

Christians have at times deliberated about the relationship between the Sabbath and Sunday. While various Christian traditions have sorted out this relationship differently, the Sabbath was originally the seventh day, the day that Jesus himself observed on Holy Saturday when he rested from his passion and death. Consider also the idea that our Jewish forebears observed a day's beginning neither at dawn nor at midnight, but at sunset. Recall the foundational creation story: the first chapter of the Bible says, "And there was evening and there was morning, the first day" (Genesis 1:5). The concept of a day was from evening first and then into morning. Would it make sense to you to say that the Christian Sabbath crosses from sunset on Saturday into Sunday morning and ends at Sunday's sunset? So what day are you observing the Sabbath?

Sunday is a celebration of Christ's resurrection, often called the Lord's Day. Sunday functions as both a first day and an "eighth" day, signaling the new creation, the new chapter that God has begun in Christ. God has not simply restored creation to its original state; God has done something utterly new in Christ that moves beyond the old paradigm.

However, this does not abolish the role of Sabbath-keeping or the seven-day week within Christian faith. The Sabbath for us as Christians is not only remembering the work of God in creation, but remembering God's work in re-creation through the death and resurrection of Jesus. This session emphasizes the way in which the Bible (especially the Old Testament) describes Sabbath as a time to remember God's work in creation and God's deliverance in the exodus, as well as a time for us to respond by entering into God's rest.

Do you think God is more concerned with *when* we observe the Sabbath, *whether* we observe the Sabbath, or *how* we observe it? Why?

Prepare Your Heart

+ Recent studies suggest that adolescents experience a shift in their sleep cycle that causes them to stay up later at night and need more sleep in the morning; however, some school systems begin their class days as early as 7:30 a.m. As a result, sleep deprivation is a chronic problem for many students. The Sabbath is a reminder of the merciful command of God that calls us to stop and care for our physical needs through rest. Who in your ministry seems worn out by all the stresses and strains of daily life? Jot their names here. Extend your heart to them.

- We live in a culture that places a high value on one's ability to work, leading many to equate their worth with their productivity. Students feel pressure to maintain a busy schedule packed with classes, athletics, and extracurricular activities. This emphasis on effort and achievement encourages workaholism, competition, and the illusion of autonomy. In contrast, the Sabbath invites us to stop our own work and recognize our dependency on God who sustains us. Who in your group may confuse worth with productivity? How does God sustain that person? How does God sustain you?

- Our society has grown attached to constant access — to the news, to stores, to anything that might be needed or wanted; the result is that the distinction between weekday and weekend is increasingly lost. Sabbath, however, calls us to the rhythm of "time set apart," inviting us to enter into the rest that we receive as we remember God our Creator. How can your meetings and other youth ministry functions become a "time set apart"?

- Youth ministers and leaders are not exempt from the increasing frenzy in our culture. It is important for us to consider the ways in which we also fail to respond to the call of Sabbath. Have we begun to consider our work more important than God's work in the lives of those we minister to? Are we willing to relinquish our role and let others step in so that we might rest?

Prepare Your Space

- Remove any clocks from the rooms to reduce distraction.

- Set up five areas for the stations. If possible, provide a table for each of the first four stations, and cover each table with newsprint paper. Set up Station 1 with two tall candles and a lighter or matches, as well as additional tea lights or other small candles that participants can light as they use this station. Set up Station 2 with a loaf of *challah* or other bread and grapes or other fruit. (You may want to put Station 2 outdoors; see below). Set up

Station 3 with a basin of water and towels. Set up Station 4 with a basket of small stones and permanent markers. Set up Station 5 by creating a space on the floor nearby with throw pillows so that participants can sit on the floor. If you have a large group, set more furniture and supplies for each station. Each station should also have handouts with its respective description, Scripture passage, reflection questions, instructions for the practice, and the written prayer. You may want to put several Bibles on each table so that participants can read the passages.

Prepare Your Supplies

- Basket or box to collect watches, cell phones, etc. Optional: a zip-top plastic bag for each person.
- Tables (four).
- Printed instructions for each station.
- Pens and paper or spiral notebooks (for participants to write down their thoughts and prayers).
- Bibles.
- Crayons for writing prayers on newsprint paper.
- Candles (two) and lighter or matches.
- Tea lights or other small candles (roughly one for each participant) and small paper plates if needed to catch wax drips.
- *Challah* loaves (at least two, either bought or homemade) or other loaves of bread.
- Grapes.
- Small stones in a basket.
- Permanent marker (for writing on stones).
- Basin of water and towel for handwashing.
- Pillows for rest area at Station 5.
- Bell.
- Song lyrics if needed for quiet reflective song to end worship time.
- Recording of peaceful background music to play during stations and an appropriate player.

Prepare Your Plan

This session will help participants consider the role that rest plays in their own lives. During this session, we will enter into a time that is more reflective and peaceful than our ordinary time. In the main movement of this session, participants will be invited to visit several stations that focus on various themes related to Sabbath and the stories of creation and exodus. Participants will gather at the end to close in prayer and to consider ways to incorporate rest in their lives through Sabbath practices.

Prepare Your Publicity

* Pass out samples of warm *challah* bread along with flyers inviting people to a session on Sabbath rest.

* Use the slogan: "Observe–Remember–Rest." Communicate the slogan using posters, announcements, electronics, and personal invitation. Be sure to offer details about when and where the session will occur.

Prepare in Prayer

(You are invited to make additions to make this prayer your own.)

God, Creator and King, you are the God who made creation and called it good. We thank you for providing...

Forgive us for the idolatry we commit when we try to improve on your work through our own efforts. Forgive me especially for the ways I have failed to enter into your rest...

Help me to find rest especially in the midst of...
(name situations that are stressful or difficult)

I pray that the gift of rest will be given especially to...
(name students who seem especially in need of God's rest)

I pray that creation may rest from our labors, such as...

God, as we learn about the Sabbath, give us minds that remember your past provision and hearts that delight in your good creation. We need courage to cease from our striving; help us to rest after you. Amen.

Prepare Further

- Explore Dorothy Bass's chapter on "Keeping Sabbath" in *Practicing Our Faith* as well as her book *Receiving the Day: Christian Practices for Opening the Gift of Time.*

- Learn more about Jewish practices of Sabbath at the website *www.jewfaq.org.*

- Ken Collins, a Christian Church (Disciples of Christ) pastor, has a helpful webpage entitled "Who Moved the Sabbath to Sunday?" which deals with the place of the Jewish Sabbath in Christian faith. *www.kencollins.com/question-42.htm.*

TEMPLATE FOR SESSION THIRTEEN
Entering into Sabbath Rest

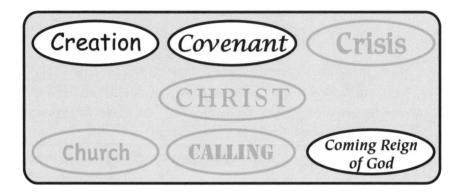

Key Scripture: Psalm 46:10

> Be still, and know that I am God!
> I am exalted among the nations,
> I am exalted in the earth.

Objectives

- To become familiar with stories in the Bible that are connected to Sabbath.

- To participate in practices inspired by God's gift of Sabbath.

- To enter into the rest intended for us as God's beloved creatures.

> Tip: Read the entire session in advance, gather materials, set up the room(s), and recruit or orient leaders. Some investment in preparation will make for a meaningful event!

Welcome (5–8 minutes)

Welcome each person who arrives. Form "journey groups" who will journey together from station to station. Appoint a leader (youth or adult) for each journey group. You may want to describe a rotation pattern and suggested time frame. For example, each journey group could begin at a different station, and then proceed clockwise around the room, staying 8 minutes at each station. Each journey group leader would decide when to migrate to a new station.

Alternative Idea: By staggering times, each group could begin with Station 1 and proceed in order. Provide a quiet resting place with soft music for the groups that finish first.

Procedural Note: To help things flow smoothly, it is suggested that you assign a host (youth or adult) to each station who will facilitate the activities there by reading the description and Scripture aloud before leading the reflection questions and observance activities. Or if you'd like shared leadership, simply have the journey group leader invite different members of her or his group to lead various activities at each station.

Explain your chosen procedures, either here or prior to beginning the station rotation.

Establish a gentle mood with soft lighting and playing or singing peaceful music. Stand before the group and smilingly *wait* for them to become attentive. Say to the group, "Welcome to this special time of receiving God's rest! So that we may focus on our wonderful God, it's important for us to be free from interruptions and worries during our time together. Sometimes it's good to be freed from time constraints and the potential of constant communications. Sometimes it's refreshing to simply be still. God's Word says, "Be still, and know that I am God! I am exalted among the nations, I am exalted in the earth" (Psalm 46:10).

"Let's say together three times the Psalm phrase 'Be still, and know that I am God' as we silence and remove our watches, placing them on the floor in front of us." (*Pause.*) "Now let's again say together three times the Psalm phrase 'Be still, and know that I am God' as we silence and remove our cell phones and other electronics, placing them on the floor in front of us, bringing all of our communication to the feet of God. (*If anyone is expecting an emergency call, for example, if a loved one is facing surgery, just speak to a leader about how to receive such a call.*)" (*Pause.*) "Now, let's close our eyes and pray the Psalm phrase three times as the leaders gather up the devices for safe keeping until after this session." (*Pause.*) Tip: You could place each person's belongings in a separate zip-top style bag.

"Continuing in an attitude of prayer, let's consider the joys and the concerns we bring that may distract us from giving our full attention to God. Let us offer them up to God, asking for peace and stillness in their place." (*Pause for about 30 seconds to let participants do so.*)

Then say, "Now I am going to read the entire verse from Psalm 46 three times. As you listen, hear God's call to stillness."

Read this verse three times, pausing dramatically between readings to let the words sink in:

> Be still, and know that I am God!
> I am exalted among the nations,
> I am exalted in the earth.

Invitation to Engagement (8–12 minutes)

Tell group members, "Now we will spend some time reflecting on how we experience rest in our own lives. I invite you to close your eyes and imagine yourself when you were younger, dozing in the car after a day of enjoyment, like at the beach or the park. Feel the sense of peaceful rest as you relax to the steady rhythm of the road. Feel the trust as you are carried or led from the car to your bedroom or another place of rest. Settle in to rest for the night. All is well. Just rest. Ahh."

Have a volunteer ready to read Exodus 20:8–11 aloud, twice if necessary.

Ask the group:

+ What specific reason does God give for observing the Sabbath?

+ What events are the people remembering when they rest?

+ Why do you think God would ask his people to take one day a week to observe the Sabbath?

Tell the group, "Our word 'Sabbath' comes from the Hebrew word *Shabbat,* which means to cease or to stop." Ask:

+ What sorts of things do people refrain from doing on the Sabbath?

+ Does your family do anything differently on Sunday?

+ What events might Christians remember during a Sabbath observance?

+ How does Sabbath shape your own life now?

Is there a particular place that invites you to rest?

Learning / Prayer Stations (25–40 minutes)

Say to the group, "We have set up stations around the room that will help you enter into Sabbath time and reflect on how the Sabbath might speak to us as God's people. At each station you will gain wisdom about Sabbath practice and have the opportunity to reflect in prayer."

Option: To begin, invite the group to sit or stand around the two candles of the "Illumination" station (page 235.)

Say something like, "God called God's people to stop working on the Sabbath so that they could spend time in other ways. In the Jewish tradition, the first step in preparing for the Sabbath celebration is lighting two candles. The two Sabbath candles at our "Illumination" station represent the two things God commanded the people of Israel to do on the Sabbath: 'Observe' and 'Remember.' We will experience the Sabbath today by *remembering* the stories behind the Sabbath, especially the creation story and the story of the Exodus out of Egypt. We will also *observe* the Sabbath by practicing ways for us to enter into Sabbath rest."

Tell the group, "At each station you will find a way to remember and a way to observe the Sabbath. At each station you will find a reading from Scripture, some reflection questions, and a symbol or activity related to the focus of that station. You may also find a prayer written to guide your own time of praying."

Orient your group to the stations, briefly explaining the purpose of each (see below pages 235–239). Otherwise, you might simply point out the location of each station and provide participants with a handout that describes each station. Give any needed instructions about journey groups, rotation, leadership, and peacefulness.

After you have done an overview of the stations, distribute a pen and paper or a spiral notebook to each participant and say, "This paper is for you to respond to the reflection questions and to write out your own prayers. Carry it with you to use at each station you visit. You will be invited to *write* your reflections in private before God, more than discuss them with one another. Because practicing Sabbath is about entering a different kind of time, in which we are able to rest before God and with one another, we will keep silence and respect each other. You may hear peaceful music in the background. You will have an opportunity to talk about your experience after we all complete our journeys to all of the stations."

Tip: To emphasize the unique peace and quiet of Sabbath, we're encouraging the reflecting and praying to be written rather than verbal. Many of our media-swamped youth will find this challenge refreshing once they experience it. However, if you feel your particular participants need the accountability of group discussion, you may certainly facilitate that. Just adjust your instructions accordingly. You know your group best.

(Option: If near the "Illumination" station, invite a participant to light the two candles.)

Say, "We will now enter into Sabbath time. Let's prepare in quietness, hearing again the invitation of Psalm 46:10. You may then begin to explore the stations. Either your journey group leader or a station host will lead and assist you at each station."

Again repeat Psalm 46:10 as in the Welcome section. Afterward dismiss participants to the stations, which are described in the handouts. Begin the peaceful background music.

> **Desired result: To enjoy rest while remembering God's creation and the Exodus.**

Re-Gathering

When most participants have completed their station visits, gather the group by ringing a bell or by beginning to sing a repetitive song that participants can join as they arrive, such as a Taizé song or a simple praise chorus.

Then pray: "O God, Creator and King, thank you for giving us the gifts of creation, deliverance, and Sabbath. Thank you for giving us time set aside for remembering who you are and who we are as your people. Keep our hearts and minds steadfast, trusting in your goodness. Help us to find ways to rest in you and to live out your Sabbath in the world. Amen."

Reflection (15–20 minutes)

Ask participants to reflect on the following questions. Form small groups of four or five to discuss each question. To maintain focus, you may want to introduce a question, give them a few minutes to discuss it as a group, and then have the groups report their thoughts to the group as a whole before moving on to the next question.

1. Which station did you enjoy the most? What Scripture or practice was most meaningful to you? Why?

2. What was it like to enter a different sort of time? In what ways was it different? How did it make you feel? How did we create "different" time?

3. These stations were focused around remembering two major events in the history of God's people: Creation and the Exodus. What attributes of God stood out to you as you remembered those events? In other words, what was noteworthy to you about who God is and what God does?

4. What did you remember during this time that you don't want to forget? What observances or practices might you want to take up regularly?

5. How do you think that Sabbath might challenge the way we currently live our lives?

6. Does Sabbath challenge any values of our culture? How?

7. What might Sabbath rest look like in the life of our youth community?

8. How might you choose to practice Sabbath?

Which influences teens more: Sabbath rest or reality TV?

Worship (7–10 minutes)

Begin by having the group sit or stand in a circle. Say something like, "Let's begin by reminding ourselves of the words of Psalm 46:10. I will say the verse once to refresh your memories, and then please join me in saying this verse as we continue to rest in the presence of God."

Slowly recite Psalm 46:10. Pause for a moment and invite participants to join you, saying, "Together let us say":

> Be still, and know that I am God!
> I am exalted among the nations,
> I am exalted in the earth.

Say to the group, "Today we have been still long enough to remember God's goodness to us. We've also seen that the people of Israel sometimes forgot God's provision and began to worry and complain. Sometimes we, like the Israelites, may not sense God's goodness; sometimes we may feel like God has abandoned us in the wilderness. Sometimes we will forget the ways that God has provided for us. However, these verses remind us that God cannot forget us":

Read aloud Isaiah 49:13–16 (we are engraved on God's palms).

Interpret or expound upon this passage for the group, saying something like, "Because it's like we are engraved on God's palms, God cannot forget us or forsake us. Sabbath practices like the ones we've experienced here help us to rest and remember all the God has done and is doing. Such rest and remembering will increase our trust in God and make our lives effective testimonies to God's power and love."

Invite participants to pray aloud any of the prayers they wrote down during the stations.

Close with a quiet song that invites God's presence and peace to enter into our lives. Examples:

- Hymn "Dear God Embracing Humankind" (*New Century Hymnal* #502), also known as "Dear Lord and Father of Mankind"

- Hymn "It Is Well"

- Taizé chant "In the Lord (I'll Be Ever Thankful)."

Closing Prayer

God, you have welcomed us into a place of rest today. We thank you for your faithfulness to provide for your people and give them good gifts from your creation. Help us to receive rest and peace from you in our hearts, souls, minds, and strength. Give us thankful hearts for all your goodness toward us. In the name of Christ. Amen.

Follow-up and Announcements

Encourage participants to continue thinking about how they might observe the Sabbath both personally and as a group. Here are some ideas for follow-up:

- Consider planning a Sabbath time at the church on a Sunday afternoon. Invite people of all ages to come and experience rest through quiet time and fellowship over a meal.

- Meet to study Sabbath practices in deeper detail; read *Receiving the Day* by Dorothy Bass together. Or you might read Lauren Winner's chapter on Sabbath in her book *Mudhouse Sabbath*. Discuss how it helps us understand the purpose of Sabbath from a Jewish and a Christian perspective.

- Enjoy God's creation as a group by going on a walk or a hike. You may want to make a portion of your hike a time for silent meditation, which you introduce by reading Genesis 1 aloud and then inviting the group to continue on silently, reflecting on creation's goodness and God's day of rest.

- Bake *challah* together and offer it to the rest of the church during fellowship hour.

- As a group, do a prayerful reading of Psalm 95 or 100. It could be in the *lectio divina* style. As you introduce the focus for each reading, invite participants to focus upon the way in which this Psalm may speak about the reality of rest and Sabbath.

- Consider inviting a person of Jewish background or faith to speak to your group about their understanding or experience of the Sabbath. Perhaps some group members could visit a Jewish home for a Shabbat dinner. Consider partnering with youth at a local synagogue to explore Sabbath further.

◆ As part of a Sabbath session, hold a poetry reading. You may want to read Denise Levertov's poems "The Avowal," "Flickering Mind," or "Altars" from her book *The Stream and the Sapphire,* which describe our need for rest before God our Creator.

Be still and know that I am God.
— Psalm 46:10

Appendix

SUPPLEMENTAL MATERIALS

Reflection

(3–5 minutes)

Take a few minutes to reflect on the last week. Think about each day. What happened in your life?

_____

_____

_____

_____

in your family?

_____

_____

_____

_____

at school or work?

_____

_____

_____

_____

with your friends?

_____

_____

_____

_____

What emotions did you feel during this last week?

_____

_____

_____

_____

SESSION TWO / HANDOUT 2

Reading the Psalms

(7–10 minutes)

Choose three or four Psalms to read. Read each one slowly. Which one relates best to how you've been feeling?

When you feel sad: Psalms 6, 42, 102, 130

When you feel angry: Psalms 13, 22, 43, 80

When you feel afraid: Psalms 23, 27, 31, 46, 57

When you feel under attack: Psalms 3, 35, 52, 56

When you feel you need God's help: Psalms 28, 54, 88, 121

When you feel lonely: Psalms 12, 22, 69, 88

When you feel jealous or envious of others: Psalms 37, 73

When you feel guilty: Psalms 25, 32, 38, 51

When outside / when you are amazed by God's creation: Psalms 8, 18, 19, 24, 29, 93, 97, 104, 136

When you've made it through a difficult time: Psalms 9, 30, 34, 116

When you feel happy or joyful: Psalms 33, 66, 92, 96, 100, 103, 118

Morning Psalms: Psalms 5, 51, 90:13–17, 95:1–7, 100

Midday Psalms: Psalms 113, 119:105–112, 121, 126

Evening Psalms: Psalms 16, 23, 74:16–23, 139:1–12, 141

Nighttime Psalms: Psalms 3, 4, 16, 31, 63:1–8, 91, 134

Praying the Psalms

(5–10 minutes)

Go back to your favorite Psalm. Reread it slowly as a prayer from you to God.

Next, write a prayer of your own. You may want to write a new prayer. Or you may want to add verses to one or more of the Psalms you read. Make the Psalms your own.

Write your prayer here or on the back of this page.

_____

_____

_____

_____

_____

_____

_____

_____

_____

_____

_____

_____

Matthew 3:13–17

Then Jesus came from Galilee
  to John at the Jordan,
    to be baptized by him.
John would have prevented him, saying,
  "I need to be baptized by you,
    and do you come to me?"

But Jesus answered him,
  "Let it be so now;
    for it is proper for us in this way to fulfill all righteousness."
Then he consented.

And when Jesus had been baptized,
  just as he came up from the water,
    suddenly the heavens were opened to him
      and he saw the Spirit of God descending like a dove
      and alighting on him.

And a voice from heaven said,
  "This is my Son,
    the Beloved,
      with whom I am well pleased."

SESSION THREE / HANDOUT 2

How is hearing and seeing a story *told* a different experience from hearing it *read* (or reading it silently yourself)?

_____

_____

What surprised you about this story?

_____

_____

What part of the story most "clicked" with you. Why?

_____

_____

Did it make a difference to spend some time learning and then telling the story of Jesus' baptism yourself? What was that like for you?

_____

_____

Do you feel differently about your own baptism now that you've embodied the story of Jesus' baptism? If so, how?

_____

_____

_____

What does it mean to go out into the world and live and act as a baptized person?

_____

_____

_____

How do you think Jesus felt when he heard the voice from heaven say, "This is my Son, the Beloved, with whom I am well pleased"? How did it make *you* feel?

_____

_____

_____

SESSION FOUR / HANDOUT 1

Group 1: Baptism

- Old Testament passages prefiguring Jesus' life and ministry: Genesis 6:5–22 and 7:11–8:5 and 8:13–19.

- Discuss: How do you think this story could prefigure something about Jesus' life, death, or resurrection?

- New Testament passages, pointing to an Old Testament "echo of Jesus": 1 Peter 3:18–21 and Romans 6:1–4.

- Question: Going under *water* and going under *ground* are similar, in that you can't breathe in either place! These passages from 1 Peter and Romans point to the double meaning of baptism: it is both a cleansing and a way to identify with the death and resurrection of Jesus. How is dying and rising again similar to the cleansing of baptism (and to the cleansing of the Great Flood)?

- Question: Throughout history, the church has often been compared to Noah's ark. It is like the ship that carries us all through the rough waters of this world toward salvation in Christ. What does church mean to you? How do you experience the gift of salvation in your own local church?

SESSION FOUR / HANDOUT 2

Group 2: Bread

- Old Testament passage prefiguring Jesus' life and ministry: Exodus 16:2–21.

- Discuss: How do you think this story could prefigure something about Jesus' life, death, or resurrection?

- New Testament passage pointing to an Old Testament "echo of Jesus": John 6:30–40.

- Question: The story from the Israelites' time in the wilderness shows how God sustained them with manna — literally giving them their daily bread. And the passage from the Gospel of John indicates that Jesus is "the true bread of heaven," which can sustain us forever. How does Jesus sustain you in your own life? What do you think Jesus meant when he said that those who come to him will never be hungry or thirsty?

- Question: When you pray the Lord's Prayer, what do you think of when you say the words, "Give us this day our daily bread"?

SESSION FOUR / HANDOUT 3

Group 3: Water

- Old Testament passage prefiguring Jesus' life and ministry: Exodus 17:1–7.

- Discuss: How do you think this story could prefigure something about Jesus' life, death, or resurrection?

- New Testament passages, pointing to an Old Testament "echo of Jesus": 1 Corinthians 10:1–4 and John 4:7–15 and 7:37–39.

- Question: In 1 Corinthians, the Apostle Paul states forthrightly that the rock that nourished the Israelites in the wilderness was Christ. And then in the Gospel of John, we see Jesus teaching that he can provide living water to all who are thirsty. What do you think he means by this "living water," and how can we receive it from him?

- Question: Do you hear the yearning in the voice of the Samaritan woman when she says to Jesus, "Sir, give me this water, so that I may never be thirsty or have to keep coming here to draw water"? What do you think her struggles are? Are they physical? emotional? spiritual? What does it mean to be thirsty anyway?

SESSION FOUR / HANDOUT 4

Advancing Echoes

One significant connection, theologically, to make is between the Old and New Testament witnesses to Jesus Christ. And that is the connection between the *Passover* (when God spared the children of the Hebrews in Egypt) and the *Crucifixion* (when Jesus died on the cross to save the world from sin and death).

- Old Testament passages prefiguring Jesus' life and ministry:

  Exodus 11:1–12:32, where the blood of the lamb provides protection during the actual Passover event.

  Leviticus 4:1–5:13 and 8:1–17, where the sacrifice of animals for the forgiveness of sin is inaugurated in Israel's history.

  Leviticus 16:1–34, where the scapegoat bears the sins of the people on the Day of Atonement.

- New Testament passages that show Jesus Christ to be the "atoning sacrifice" for humanity:

  John 1:29–36, where John the Baptist proclaims Jesus to be the Lamb of God.

  1 Corinthians 5:7–8, where the Apostle Paul calls Jesus "our Passover" or "our paschal lamb."

  Hebrews 2:9 and 9:11–15, where Jesus' death is shown to put to an end the repeated animal sacrifices and serves as the "once for all" sacrifice to bring us to redemption.

  1 Peter 1:17–21, where Jesus is compared to the lamb "without defect or blemish."

  1 John 2:1–2, where Jesus is named as the "atoning sacrifice for our sins, and not for ours only but also for the whole world."

Revelation 5:6–17, where John's vision of the end times depicts Jesus as the Lamb who was slain as a ransom for people from all tribes and nations on the earth.

- Question: Have you ever thought about Jesus' death on the cross and its biblical connection to the Passover in the book of Exodus? The word used in the New Testament is "atonement," which is sometimes described as "at-one-ment" meaning that it is the act by which Jesus makes us one with God. How does Jesus' death on the cross draw us close to God?

- Question: Think about the experience of taking Holy Communion in the context of worship. Do any of the words or images of the Lord's Supper remind you of any of the Old Testament or New Testament passages you just read? Try going to Luke 22:14–23 to read the story of the Last Supper. Notice how Jesus mentions the Passover, how he speaks of his body given for his disciples, and how he says the cup poured out brings about a new covenant in his own blood. Does this scene help you think about the connections between the Passover and the Crucifixion?

SESSION FIVE / HANDOUT 1

Psalm 8

Enjoy reading Psalm 8.

To start noticing and discussing:

◆ What words catch your interest?

_____

_____

_____

◆ How do the words paint a picture or set a scene?

_____

_____

_____

◆ What can we learn about God by looking at the sky? the earth? animals? humans?

_____

_____

_____

_____

◆ Why does it matter that God is the Creator of all things?

_____

_____

_____

_____

◆ How is God praised in this poem?

_____

_____

_____

_____

SESSION FIVE / HANDOUT 2

Psalm 19

Enjoy Psalm 19.

The first six verses of this Psalm are an excellent and persuasive example of natural theology, as the writer deftly uses personification to characterize Creator and creation. The action verbs of "tell," "proclaim," "pour," and "declare" are a fourfold synthetic parallel, and it is striking that they are attributed to the creation, though it is as if they are echoing the Creator. All one has to do is look up and listen to what one sees, a clever use of synesthesia to witness God's artistic skill. From sunrise to sunset, through the clouds and beyond the horizon, a hymn is being sung to God at all times. (This reminds me of the song of all creation in Madeline L'Engle's *A Wrinkle in Time*, which the humans must learn to hear and some never notice.) What are we to do with verse 3 as translated in the NRSV, as it seems to contradict the previous two verses? Is the lack of speech or words literal, meaning that a figurative ear is required (see Keats's "Ode on a Grecian Urn" for the Romantic sensibility related to such hearing). Is their voice not heard because few are listening rightly? Perhaps they hear only static when they should hear music. Part of the confusion is alleviated with the NIV translation ("There is no speech or language where their voice is not heard"), which implies that all speech and all language (literal or figurative) is saturated with the sounds of creation and Creator.

SESSION FIVE / HANDOUT 2
(continued)

To start noticing and discussing:

• What words catch your interest?

_____

_____

_____

_____

_____

_____

• How do the words paint a picture or set a scene?

_____

_____

_____

_____

_____

• How is God praised in this poem?

_____

_____

_____

_____

_____

SESSION FIVE / HANDOUT 3
Psalm 104

Enjoy the poetry of Psalm 104!

To start noticing and discussing:

• What words catch your interest?

_____

_____

_____

_____

• How do the words paint a picture or set a scene?

_____

_____

_____

_____

• How is God praised in this poem?

_____

_____

_____

_____

Psalm 148

Praise the Lord while reading Psalm 148.

To start noticing and discussing:

◆ What words catch your interest?

_____

_____

_____

_____

◆ How do the words paint a picture or set a scene?

_____

_____

_____

_____

◆ How is God praised in this poem?

_____

_____

_____

_____

◆ How might all of creation praise God? angels? stars and planets? water? mountains and valleys? animals? humans?

_____

_____

_____

_____

God's Grandeur
Gerard Manley Hopkins (1844–89)

The world is charged with the grandeur of God,
    It will flame out, like shining from shook foil;
    It gathers to a greatness, like the ooze of oil
Crushed. Why do men then now not reck* his rod?
Generations have trod, have trod, have trod;
    And all is seared with trade; bleared, smeared with toil;
    And wears man's smudge and shares man's smell: the soil
Is bare now, nor can foot feel, being shod.

And for all this, nature is never spent;
    There lives the dearest freshness deep down things;
And though the last lights off the black West went
    Oh, morning, at the brown brink eastward, springs —
Because the Holy Ghost over the bent
    World broods with warm breast and with ah! bright wings.

  • How is the world "charged" with God's grandeur?

  • How have we stomped ("trod") on God's creation?

  • How is nature renewed?

---

*Note: "reck" in line 4 is similar to "reckon": to have care, concern, or regard for; to take heed of.

A Something in a Summer's Day
Emily Dickinson (1830–86)

A something in a summer's day
As slow her flambeaux burn away,
Which solemnizes me.

A something in a summer's noon, —
An azure depth, a wordless tune,
Transcending ecstasy.

And still within a summer's night
A something so transporting bright,
I clap my hands to see;

Then veil my too inspecting face,
Lest such a subtle, shimmering grace
Flutter too far for me.

The wizard-fingers never rest,
The purple brook within the breast
Still chafes its narrow bed;

Still rears the East her amber flag,
Guides still the sun along the crag
His caravan of red,

Like flowers that heard the tale of dews
But never deemed the dripping prize
Awaited their low brows;

Or bees, that thought the summer's name
Some rumor of delirium
No summer could for them;

Or Arctic creature, dimly stirred
By tropic hint, — some travelled bird
Imported to the wood;

Or wind's bright signal to the ear,
Making that homely and severe,
Contented, known, before

The heaven unexpected came,
To lives that thought their worshiping
A too presumptuous psalm.

- What might the "something" found be?
- What might "shimmering grace" look like?
- Ask a neighbor what "shimmering grace" stirs up within him or her? A memory, a hope, a pain...
- How has heaven come to you unexpectedly?

Pied Beauty
Gerard Manley Hopkins (1844–89)

Glory be to God for dappled things—
   For skies of couple-colour as a brinded* cow;
     For rose-moles all in stipple upon trout that swim;
Fresh-firecoal chestnut-falls; finches' wings;
   Landscape plotted and pieced—fold, fallow, and plough;
   And all trades, their gear and tackle and trim.

All things counter, original, spare, strange;
   Whatever is fickle, freckled (who knows how?)
     With swift, slow; sweet, sour; adazzle, dim;
He fathers-forth whose beauty is past change:
                      Praise Him.

- What might this poem show us about creation?

- What might this poem teach us about God the Creator?

- What does it invite us to ponder?

- What Scriptures connect to this poem for you?

Note: "brinded" in line 2 is similar to "brindled": gray or tawny with darker streaks or spots.

SESSION SIX / HANDOUT 1

Prayer over the Baptismal Waters

This prayer is attributed to Sophronios of Jerusalem (A.D. 600).

Today the grace of the Holy Spirit in the form of a dove dwelt upon the waters.

Today the Sun that never sets has dawned and the world is made radiant with the light of the Lord.

Today the Moon with its radiant beams sheds light on the world.

Today the stars formed of light make the inhabited world lovely with the brightness of their splendor.

Today the clouds rain down from heaven the shower of justice for mankind.

Today the Uncreated by his own will accepts the laying on of hands by his own creature.

Today the Prophet and Forerunner draws near but stands by with fear seeing God's condescension toward us.

Today the streams of Jordan are changed into healing by the presence of the Lord.

Today all creation is watered by mystical streams.

Today the failings of mankind are being washed away by the waters of Jordan.

Today Paradise is opened for mortals and the Sun of justice shines down on us.

Today the bitter water as once for Moses' people is changed to sweetness by the presence of the Lord.

Today we have been delivered from the ancient grief and saved as the new Israel.

Today we have been redeemed from darkness and are filled with radiance by the light of the knowledge of God.

Today the gloomy fog of the world is cleansed by the manifestation of our God.

Today all creation shines with light from on high.

Today error has been destroyed and the coming of the Master makes for us a way of salvation.

Today things on high keep festival with those below, and those below commune with those on high.

Today the sacred and triumphant festal assembly of the Orthodox exults.

Today the Master hastens toward baptism, that he may lead humanity to the heights.

Today the One who does not bow bows down to his own servant, that he may free us from servitude.

Today we have purchased the Kingdom of heaven, for the Kingdom of the Lord will have no end.

Today earth and sea share the joy of the world, and the world has been filled with gladness.

The waters saw you, O God, the waters saw you and were afraid.

The Jordan turned back when it saw the fire of the godhead descending in bodily form and entering it.

The Jordan turned back as it contemplated the Holy Spirit in the form of a dove, descending and flying about you.

The Jordan turned back as it saw the Invisible made visible, the Creator made flesh, the Master in the form of a servant.

The Jordan turned back and the mountains leapt as they saw God in the flesh, and the clouds uttered their voice, marveling at what had come to pass, seeing Light from Light, true God from true God, the Master's festival today in Jordan; seeing him drowning the death from disobedience, the goad of error and the bond of Hell in Jordan and granting the Baptism of salvation to the world.

Therefore I, too, a sinner and your unworthy servant, recount the greatness of your wonders and, seized with fear, in compunction cry out to you.

SESSION NINE / HANDOUT 1

Creation

• How does Eucharist enact the goodness of God's creation?

_____

_____

_____

_____

• How does Eucharist enact our own role as stewards of that creation?

_____

_____

_____

_____

• Read Psalm 34:8 aloud.

• How does Eucharist invite us to "taste and see" God's goodness?

_____

_____

_____

_____

• Why do you think we are invited to taste and see instead of God simply explaining everything to us?

_____

_____

_____

_____

Covenant

+ What are some stories of Old Testament Covenant? What signs were used to enact those covenants? (For examples, see Genesis 9:8–17 and Genesis 17:1–12.)

_____

_____

_____

_____

+ Read aloud Luke 22:20.
+ If a covenant is a binding of God to human beings, how is this binding being accomplished through Eucharist?

_____

_____

_____

_____

+ What does this Eucharistic covenant mean for our life together?

_____

_____

_____

_____

+ Does Eucharist call us to shed blood for one another? If so, when? If not, why not?

_____

_____

_____

_____

SESSION NINE / HANDOUT 3

Crisis

• Read Hebrews 9:1–14. What is the role of blood in rituals of purification?

_____

_____

_____

• How does this connect to Eucharist?

_____

_____

_____

• How is worship different now from the time of the portable tents?

_____

_____

_____

• Read Luke 22:14–34. What crises are evident?

_____

_____

_____

• What connections do you see to Eucharist?

_____

_____

_____

• How is the theological theme of crisis evident in your world today?

_____

_____

_____

Christ

- Read aloud 1 Corinthians 5:7.

- What Old Testament Story does this passage recall? (See Exodus 12:1–13.) What are the similarities and differences between the Passover lamb of the Exodus story and Jesus as the new paschal lamb?

_____

_____

_____

- What do these have to do with Eucharist?

_____

_____

_____

- Read aloud Luke 24:30–31.

- What does the fact that the disciples recognized Jesus as resurrected and in their presence at the breaking of the bread say about the Eucharist?

_____

_____

_____

- Does our congregation emphasize more Jesus as sacrificial lamb or Jesus as alive in our midst during Eucharist? Why do you think this is so?

_____

_____

_____

Church

- Read aloud 1 Corinthians 10:16–17.

- According to this text, where does the church find its identity?

_____

_____

_____

_____

- In your opinion, does Eucharistic sharing of bread and drink in our church highlight or mask the unity of the church as one body in Christ?

_____

_____

_____

_____

- What would you do differently if you were in charge?

_____

_____

_____

_____

SESSION NINE / HANDOUT 6

Calling

• Read aloud 1 Corinthians 11:20–22.

• What seems to be the problem in the Corinthian church's celebration of Eucharist?

_____

_____

_____

_____

_____

• What does the Eucharist intend with respect to the distribution of food?

_____

_____

_____

_____

_____

• How does our Eucharistic meal point to specific Christian callings to serve God and world?

_____

_____

_____

_____

_____

SESSION NINE / HANDOUT 7

Coming Reign of God

- Read aloud Luke 14:12–14.

- How is this story a "foretaste" of God's promised Reign?

_____

_____

_____

_____

_____

- Does our congregation's celebration resemble this portrait? Why or why not?

_____

_____

_____

_____

- If not what are we called to do about it?

_____

_____

_____

_____

The Origins of the Christian Pattern of Time

In the beginning, God gave Israel the *Week*.

- For six days God worked on creation (Genesis 1).

- The seventh ("Sabbath") day, God rested and enjoyed what God had made (Genesis 2:2).

- God commands that Israel also work six days and rest on the seventh (Exodus 20:8–11; 31:12–17).

Theological Implications of Observing the Week

- God is *Creator* and creation is a good gift. Human beings are part of that good creation.

- For Israel to keep Sabbath sustains the memory of God's good gift of creation and gratitude for that gift.

- Six days of work and a Sabbath day of rest invite both the labor that tends God's creation *and* rest from that work as a sign that God's providential care continues even when human beings do not work. God is *sustainer* of our lives. We are creatures dependent upon God.

Summary

To pattern time by the seven-day week means God is *Creator* and creation is good; God *delivers* persons from oppression and despair; God *sustains* all life including human life.

Soon God gave Israel the Festival of the *Passover.*

On this night Jews commemorate:

- God remembering Israel's oppression (Exodus 3).

- God sparing Israel's firstborn by "passing over" their households (Exodus 11–12:13).

- God the *deliverer* freeing them from slavery in Egypt and bringing them through the Red Sea (Exodus 13:17–14:31).

- God's command to celebrate the Passover annually (Deuteronomy 16:1–8; Exodus 12:14–27).

Theological Implications of Keeping Passover

- God hears the cries of the suffering and the oppressed.

- God delivers persons, communities, and all creation out of bondage.

- God makes and keeps promises.

- God continues to work in the world for liberation and freedom.

To the Church, God Gave a *New Day*

Many New Testament Christians were Jews. They kept the seven-day week and practiced the Sabbath. Soon they also assembled for worship at dawn of the first day of the week. This day came to be known as:

- The *Lord's* Day — A weekly marking of the day of Christ's resurrection from the dead (Matthew 28:1–6; Acts 20:7; Revelation 1:10).

- The *Eighth* Day — A playful association of all the themes of creation in the seven-day week to the new thing God is doing in Jesus Christ (Colossians 1:13–20).

- *Sun*-day — Christ is the true light of the world who made the sun and outshines its glory (Malachi 4:2; John 1:1–5; Revelation 21:23).

Theological Implications of Worship on the Lord's Day

- Christ's resurrection is the central experience of the church. Nothing is more important to Christian faith (1 Corinthians 15:12–19). That is why the church marks the Lord's resurrection weekly.

- Christ's resurrection inaugurates a "new creation." All things under heaven are refashioned through him. Creation is renewed.

- The prophet in the book of Revelation sees a day when God's Reign is fulfilled: that the world will no longer need the sun "for the glory of God is its light, and its lamp is the Lamb." Thus worship on Sunday also provides a foretaste of Christ's Reign.

God Also Gave the Church *Pascha*

By the second century, the church began to celebrate a great yearly Lord's Day. In North America, this day is called "Easter." But throughout most of the world, the church calls the day by its more ancient name, *Pascha,* meaning "Passover." This is partly because the Christian *Pascha* has always been celebrated close to the Jewish Passover and partly because the meanings of Israel's Passover and the Christian *Pascha* are so intertwined. What began as a single day to commemorate Jesus' life, death, and resurrection quickly morphed into multiple days, called the "Triduum" (Good Friday, Holy Saturday, Easter Sunday). We know through the writings of Egeria, a fourth-century pilgrim to Jerusalem, that, in addition to the Triduum, the church in that city practiced an entire Holy Week marking the final days before Jesus' crucifixion.

Theological Implications of the Yearly Celebration of Pascha

* The church recognized in Jesus the new Passover lamb (1 Corinthians 5:7–8). Similar to Israel's understanding of its own Passover festival, the church professes that Christ's death saves us from God's judgment, his resurrection delivers us from slavery to sin and death, and his life and ministry show us the way into the new "Promised Land" of God's Reign.

* *Pascha* quickly grew from one day each year to three days, to a week to an entire season that spans seven weeks to the Day of Pentecost. Not coincidentally, as the Lord's Day is one-seventh of the week, the season of *Pascha* (Easter) is one-seventh of the year. In its inspiration the church recognized that a gift as extraordinary as Christ's resurrection must be dwelt upon and celebrated for more than a single day.

Finally, the Church Received the Entire *Christian Year*

By the fourth century, the seven-week long Season of Easter along with its intimate connection to the Day of Pentecost (marking the gift of the Holy Spirit as with tongues of fire) was firmly established. In addition, Lent, forty days of preparation for baptism or renewal of baptism into the life, death, and resurrection of Jesus Christ at Easter, was begun. The cycle from ashes to fire (Lent, Easter, Pentecost) was now complete.

In a similar manner, seasons of Advent, Christmas, the Day of Epiphany, and the season after Epiphany soon developed as well. The first major festival was the Day of Epiphany (meaning "manifestation") marking Jesus' baptism and God's announcement of his identity ("This is my Son, the Beloved"; Matthew 3:17) to the world. This day became associated with other celebrations of God being made manifest: Jesus' birth; his circumcision; the visit from the magi; and his first public miracles. As with *Pascha*, a single day became a cluster of days and finally a group of seasons: Advent, Christmas concluding with the Day of Epiphany, and the Season after Epiphany. By the end of the fourth century the cycle from hope to joy is also complete.

Theological Implications of the Patterning of the Christian Year

- The chronology of this development — first the Lord's Day, next the annual Great Lord's Day (*Pascha*), then the full season of Easter and its attending seasons and days followed by Epiphany and the seasons attending Epiphany — demonstrates the early church's judgment about its most important theological convictions. Nothing was more central than the resurrection. Marking it weekly also enacted the church's belief that the risen Christ, now in the power of the Holy Spirit, continued to be present in her midst. Stretching the yearly Great Lord's Day into a Holy Week soon brought proper attention to the significance of Jesus' death. Yet the One who died and rose also lived a life of consequence, thus the equally understandable (and inspired) desire to attend to dimensions of Christ's life and ministry by way of Christmas and Epiphany.

- The Christian Year is implicitly Trinitarian. The creative activity of *God* is made manifest at Epiphany, especially at Jesus' baptism and the inauguration of the New Creation. Through his life, death, and resurrection, enacted most fully at Lent, Holy Week, and Easter, *Jesus Christ* offers salvation and deliverance from sin and oppression. The entire Easter Season concluding with Pentecost communicates the implications of the gift of the *Spirit* for sustaining the church toward the completion of God's Reign.

- The Christian Pattern of Time is an invitation to participate in the drama of God's salvation of the world. The Lord's Day and other holy days and seasons do not merely commemorate past events, they invite us to see God at work in the present shaping the future.

SESSION 12 / HANDOUT 2

Discussion Questions

♦ Read Genesis 1:5, Genesis 2:2, and Exodus 20:8–11. What evidence do the Scriptures contain pointing to the origins of the Christian Pattern of Time?

♦ Much of the Christian Year developed fully only after the era of the church of the New Testament. How should Christians evaluate the Christian Pattern of Time in light of this fact? For example, is the Christian Pattern of Time faithful to the Gospels or does it detract from or distort them?

♦ From what you have read, what seems to be the relationship between Jewish and Christian calendars? How does this relationship impact your thinking about your own Christian faith?

♦ What does the Christian Pattern of Time suggest about the relationship between theological beliefs we know in our heads and convictions we carry in our bodies? Is one way of knowing more authentic, more truthful than the other?

_____

_____

♦ How attentive is our congregation to the Christian Patterning of Time?

_____

_____

♦ Which holy days or seasons seem to be emphasized? Which are diminished or left out entirely? To what effect?

_____

_____

♦ What can we do about it?

_____

_____

SESSION 13 / HANDOUT 1

Station 1: Illumination

Description

Of all the things God could have created first, God created light. In the Exodus, God appeared as a pillar of fire, a light to guide the Israelites through the dark wilderness after they fled from slavery in Egypt. At this station we ask for divine light to shine in areas of our lives where we need guidance or wisdom.

Remember

Read Genesis 1:1–5 (God creates light and calls it good)

Read Exodus 13:17–22 (God as the pillar of fire)

Reflection Questions

- What can we learn about God's character from God's decision to create light first?
- What parts of life that seem dark or difficult to you right now need to be flooded with God's light?

Observe/Practice

Light a candle. If possible, let each person light a candle. As the lighting occurs, give each person an opportunity to whisper (with just one or two words) a situation that either shows or needs God's light. Example: "God, I pray that you will shine your light on...." [Add situations or individuals that need the illumination of God's light.]

Prayer

God, Creator and King, we remember that light was your very first creation. We light these candles and ask that you might shine your light into our hearts during this Sabbath time. Let your light be seen by all.

Station 2: Feasting on the Fruit of Creation

Description

In creation, God made the natural world a bountiful place where humans could flourish and be sustained. In the Exodus, when the Israelites were wandering in the wilderness, God provided food from heaven and water from rocks for them. At this station we remember the ways that we as humans receive God's blessing through the gifts of the earth.

Remember

Read Genesis 1:11–13; Genesis 1:27–30 (God creates the earth's vegetation as food for humankind).

Read Exodus 16:10–18 (God's gift of manna in the wilderness).

Reflection Questions

• What attributes of God do we discover as we remember God's gifts of provision in the biblical accounts of creation and exodus?

• When have you seen God reflected in the created world?

Observe/Practice

Invite participants to quietly enjoy some bread and grapes, first saying a prayer of thanksgiving or blessing over the food.

Prayer

God, Creator and King, thank you for the gifts of the earth that we too often take for granted. Thank you for this food set before me and for those who harvested it. Thank you for this reminder that we live and move and have our being because of you and your generosity. I pray that you will help us to remember that you are . . . " [add characteristics of God revealed in these stories].

SESSION 13 / HANDOUT 1
(continued)

Station 3: Remember Deliverance

Description

The Israelites experienced many powerful acts of God as God led them out of Egypt toward the Promised Land. One way that they remembered their history with God was to pile stones as a memorial at a place where God had delivered them. At this station we make a memorial to help us remember what God has done for us.

Remember

Read Exodus 18:7–12 (rejoicing over God's deliverance).

Read Joshua 3:14–4:9 (crossing of the Jordan and memorial stones).

Reflection Questions

- What were the Israelites trying to remember when they piled up stones?
- What is a modern-day parallel to making a pile of stones?
- How might you keep God's mighty acts fresh and alive in your mind and heart?

Observe/Practice

Take a stone from the basket and write on it a word or phrase that reminds you of God's gracious action on your behalf. Then add it to the pile being created at the station as you complete the sentence, "I thank God for helping [or delivering me] when _____."

Prayer

God, Creator and King, you are faithful to deliver your people in times of need. God, help me to remember that you are the God who delivered your people from slavery. I remember times when you delivered my family [or friend or church or country] from . . . " [add events or stories of God's deliverance from your own experience].

Station 4: Purification

Description

Even though God provided everything that the Israelites needed in the wilderness, they often forgot and began to complain against God. Even though God brought them out of slavery in Egypt, when Pharaoh showed up at the bank of the Red Sea, the people were afraid and did not trust in God. The Sabbath is about remembering God as the giver of all good things. We are easily distracted from remembering that our lives are a gift from God, and we often fail to enter into Sabbath rest. At this station we confess the ways in which we have failed to live in God's rest, and we ask to be cleansed and made whole by God's mercy.

Remember

Read Exodus 14:10–21 (the Israelites speak against God; God saves).

Reflection Questions

◆ In what situations has it been difficult for you to trust in God?

◆ What failure to trust or enter into rest do you need to confess to God?

Observe/Practice

Confess any sin you may be aware of. Dip your hands in the water to represent God's forgiveness and washing away of sin. Just as God brought the Israelites through the waters of the Red Sea even though they complained and doubted, remember that God will be faithful to provide for you, even when you complain or doubt.

Prayer

God, Creator and King, you have offered us an amazing gift in giving us life, the earth, and the Sabbath. I confess to you that I have thought of my time as my own, instead of as a gift from you. Please forgive me and help me to trust that you will continue to provide for me as I deal with . . . " [add concerns].

Station 5: Rest

Description

Psalm 46 reminded us that we are called to silence before God. Restful quiet is part of keeping Sabbath. After God created light, the earth, its fruit and humankind, God rested, not because God was bored or indifferent, but because creation was complete. God desires for people to enter into rest, trusting in God's provision and goodness. At this station we do this through a time of quiet, meditative prayer.

Remember

Read Genesis 1:31–2:3 (God finishes creation and rests).

Read Exodus 31:12–17 (God commands the Sabbath).

Reflection Questions

- What worries might hold you back from entering God's rest?
- How might God's decision to rest on the seventh day encourage you to relinquish those concerns?

Observe/Practice

Choose a simple, peaceful word to dwell on, such as "peace," *shalom* ("peace/wholeness" in Hebrew), "Jesus," or "light." Find a seat in the rest area and get comfortable; then close your eyes, breathe deeply and slowly repeat this word, either whispering it or silently. Release any tension from your body and relax. Enter into a time of rest, letting go of worries or concerns that might distract you. Your leader will close your time at this station with a prayer. (One possible prayer is printed below.)

Prayer

> *God, Creator and King, I relinquish myself to your love and your care. Help me to rest after you, knowing that you are our Provider and Deliverer. I rest in the shadow of your wings.*

About the Duke Youth Academy for Christian Formation

Katherine Smith

The Duke Youth Academy for Christian Formation is a summer program for selected high school students to live in an intentional Christian community on the campus of Duke University in Durham, North Carolina.

Days at the Youth Academy are patterned by worship of God through word and sacrament, reflection on Scripture, service and table fellowship, rest and play — practices ancient and modern that nourish the life of faith in Christ. In Christian community, Youth Academy participants study theology with Duke Divinity School faculty, explore the arts with professional artists-in-residence, and practice faith through hospitality, servant ministry, prayer, reconciliation, and small group reflection.

The academy is open to applications from rising juniors and seniors in high school from any Christian tradition. Through the Lilly Endowment, Inc., all accepted students receive a tuition scholarship. Detailed information on room and board fees for the two weeks during the upcoming summer is available on the DYA website. Financial aid is available.

In addition to the summer academy, DYA offers numerous resources to strengthen youth ministry and train youth workers within churches and judicatories. Each summer, the academy invites several youth workers to journey alongside the DYA community through the Ministry Fellowship. For one week, Fellows participate fully in the Duke Youth Academy, exploring DYA's approach to youth ministry and reflecting on their own vocation working with young people. A midyear retreat offers bread for the continuing journey of faith as past participants gather to worship and explore ways to live out their gifts for leadership and service in Christ.

The Youth Academy also offers traveling seminars and tailored programming for congregations and denominational gatherings (district, conference, diocese, presbytery, synod, etc.) These events range from one- or two-hour teaching sessions to multiday events led by veteran DYA staff members. New programs are always being envisioned to fortify you and your youth ministry. Duke Divinity School now offers a Master of Arts in Christian Practice degree with a focus on youth ministry. This program includes both on-campus intensives and on-line components.

To learn more about the Duke Youth Academy for Christian Formation or to inquire about hosting a seminar for your group or event, please contact:

> Duke Youth Academy for Christian Formation
> 312 Blackwell Street, Suite 101
> Durham, NC 27701
> 919-613-5323
> *duyouth@div.duke.edu*

Contributors

Sarah Arthur's gift with words is evident in her books, including *Walking with Frodo, Dating Mr. Darcy,* and *The God-Hungry Imagination.* Seven years as a youth director led to a master's degree in North Carolina; then she returned to Michigan, where it's much colder! Discover more about her speaking and writing at her website, *saraharthur.com.*

Liz DeGaynor brought her experience as an English teacher to her ministry with teens at DYA. A master's degree couldn't quench her zest for learning; she's pursuing a doctoral degree now. Her interest in poetry makes her an excellent conversation partner.

Rev. Dr. Fred Edie has been a youth minister in California and Georgia, and he now teaches youth ministry, Christian education, and practical theology at Duke Divinity School. He is faculty director of the Duke Youth Academy for Christian Formation (DYA.) He loves cycling, for transportation and recreation.

Rev. Brian Hardesty-Crouch is chaplain and spiritual director for DYA. As president of *holymoments.org,* he writes, teaches, and leads retreats about Christian spirituality. A member of Spiritual Directors International, he's also on the faculty of HeartPaths Spirituality Centre DFW in Texas. Brian has enjoyed countless pizza "dinners" during more than twenty years of youth ministry.

Rev. Sarah Kerr served as a mentor for a covenant group at DYA and continued in youth ministry as an Episcopal priest in Florida before relocating in Tennessee. Her session on Sabbath was the first one written for this book. Can you smell the bread baking?

Laurea Glusman McAllister helped advance the ministries of hospitality for DYA while earning dual degrees in social work (University of North Carolina) and theology (Duke). Working as a youth minister led her to become a counselor at an agency specializing in eating disorder treatment. Laurea likes to garden, cook, and sing.

Dr. Tracy Radosevic shares the gift of biblical storytelling with churches and conferences around the United States and beyond. She has been a leader in the Network of Biblical Storytellers and also teaches at Wesley Theological Seminary in Washington, D.C. *Tracyrad.com* is based in Maryland. Tracy is often an artist-in-residence at DYA, helping teenagers let the Bible come alive.

Rev. Dr. Matt Schlimm is assistant professor of Old Testament in Dubuque, Iowa. He is a lover of coffee and chicken scaloppini, and his great laugh makes everyone at the table feel welcome. He's interested in the importance of emotion in ethical living. Matt, a United Methodist pastor, has served churches in Michigan, Minnesota, and North Carolina. He led a prayer practice at DYA on "Praying the Psalms."

Rev. Katherine Smith came to Durham from Nashville via Princeton. She served as the assistant director of DYA and handled the myriad logistics of both staff and students with grace and professionalism. She burns off the stress with a good run.

Meredith Stewart, with degrees in both law and theology, now devotes her energy to teaching school for early adolescents. As service and hospitality coordinator for DYA, she led students and staff to new experiences in justice ministries. Meredith has also shared her gifts with teenagers as a youth director for an Episcopal church.

Rev. Andrew Thompson has served as coordinator of the Arts Village and Christian Practices at DYA. A frequent blogger and contributor to the United Methodist Reporter (*umportal.org*), he was pastor of a rural church while working on a doctoral degree at Duke. Andrew loves many things, including Arkansas!